WINNING THE INVESTMENT MARATHON

A Simple Path to Financial Success

WINNING THE INVESTMENT MARATHON

A Simple Path to Financial Success

H. Bradlee Perry

THE MIDAS PRESS

Published in 1999 by The Midas Press
Upton, MA

First Printing, 1999

ISBN 0-9673138-0-5

Library of Congress Catalog Card Number: 99-73441

*To all investors, young and old, experienced
and inexperienced, individual and professional.
May your investment marathon be as rewarding
and enjoyable as mine has been.*

CONTENTS

ACKNOWLEDGMENTS

N IH (not invented here) is just as unproductive an attitude in investing as in most other activities. I have learned much from other investors over the years. Astute people like Warren Buffett and David Dreman have provided many useful insights to me, and I am greatly indebted to my colleagues at David L. Babson & Co. for their contributions over the past four decades.

David L. Babson, one of the greatest investors of the twentieth century, stands out. Also invaluable to me have been my Babson associates Nick Safford, Leonard Johnson, Bill Williams, Nick Whitridge, Peter Thompson, Ted Martin, Peter Schliemann, Dutch Treat, and Brian Reynolds. (The ideas expressed in this book, however, may not be fully in accord with the current or future views of David L. Babson & Co.)

For many years I have had close and stimulating relationships with Edward Jones, the unique and very capable brokerage firm that follows most of the principles espoused in this book in serving individual investors; the American Association of Individual Investors, which does an excellent job educating its members; and the National Association of Investors Corporation, which assists the vast number of investment clubs so well. Each of these organizations has supplemented my own experience with many valuable examples of real-life investing, where final decisions are made.

All the work that ultimately produced this book was aided immeasurably over three decades by Mary Manley, Jean Tierney, and Barbara Bosworth. Special thanks to them for their unstinting efforts.

Finally, kudos to my wife for her long, loyal support of my career, which often impinged on our personal life—right up through the completion of this book.

BRAD PERRY
Cambridge, MA
July 1999

PART I

LEARNING FROM BIG WINNERS

Chapter 1

THE KEYS
TO SUCCESS

In rural Maine, the best compliment one can pay a person is not "he's really smart"—it's "he's really sensible."

The same view applies to investing. Most of the truly successful investors—Benjamin Graham, Rowe Price, David Babson, Claude Rosenberg, John Neff, Warren Buffett, John Templeton, Peter Lynch, David Dreman, and Ralph Wanger, among others—have grounded their strategies in plain common sense. They have recognized what they can do and what they cannot do. They have based their decisions on the lessons of history and on facts, not on estimates or guesses. They have been rational, not emotional, and they have stuck to their proven approaches with superb discipline.

Investing is not easy, but it is pursued most successfully in a simple, straightforward way. Those who use complicated approaches or constantly shift their strategies usually get less favorable results. The old English phrase, "too clever by half," applies well to these "smart" investors; they generally end up outsmarting themselves.

In a 1998 talk to University of Washington students, Warren Buffett, the most successful investor in history, put it this way:

"How I got here is pretty simple. . . . It's not IQ. . . . The big thing is rationality. I always look at IQ and talent as representing the horsepower of the motor, but that the output—the efficiency with which that motor works—depends on rationality. A lot of people start out with 400-horsepower motors, but only get 100 horsepower of output. It's way better to have a 200-horsepower motor and get it all into output.

"So why do smart people do things that interfere with getting the output they're entitled to? It gets into the habits and character and temperament, and behaving in a rational manner."

The investment approach recommended in this book is based on nearly 50 years of personal experience as a security analyst and portfolio manager, and on as many years' observation of other investment managers, successful and unsuccessful.

Experience and history are great teachers. All investment managers make mistakes. I've made plenty, and even Warren Buffett has had poor results with a few holdings, like USAir—but successful investors learn from their mistakes and usually do not repeat them.

As Aldous Huxley put it, "Experience is not what happens to you; it's what you do with what happens to you." In the same vein, one of the outstanding investment thinkers of the mid-1900s, Gerald M. Loeb, said: "Knowledge born from actual experience is the answer to why one profits; lack of it is the reason one loses."

Careful planning and a sound strategy are just as important in investing as in any business venture. Winning investors have a clear sense of direction and they change course only when there is a compelling reason.

This book is aimed primarily at individual investors—both those who manage their own assets and those who utilize professional help, either through an investment advisor or mutual funds. But most of the ideas expressed here can be equally useful for professional investment managers.

Using simple *common sense* is the primary theme running through the book. Also key is the need to view everything involved in investment decision making *in long-term perspective*. That isn't easy in today's conditions of information overload, intense focus on the news of the moment, and pressure for short-term performance—but the investor who fails to lift his or her eyes to the horizon regularly will not enjoy a safe and successful voyage over the constantly changing and occasionally rough seas of the stock market.

Often I'll refer to investment history—events that took place years ago, to younger people seemingly in the Dark Ages. Knowing this history is invaluable, because in investing many patterns recur and there is very little that is truly new. This gives an edge to the experienced investor who has "seen it all," but newer investors can tap into that experience by reading about the past (as in this book, I hope) and by talking to older investors. As Ralph Waldo Emerson said, "The years teach much that the days never knew."

This book is briefer than most of those written on serious subjects, including investing, because I believe the essential factors for investment success are quite simple and that investors should focus on a few basic principles. Complexity breeds confusion—and often failure—in this seemingly volatile, difficult field. To many people, investing looks complicated and scary. After reading this book, I hope you'll see that it doesn't have to be either.

PART II

STOCKS:
The Primary Source of Wealth

Chapter 2

ALL THAT
REALLY COUNTS

For most investors, common stocks are the primary means of building capital. Yet, there's a widespread misunderstanding of *why* they work so well in a sensibly planned investment program.

When you ask people what is the most important characteristic of the stock market, many will answer that it constantly fluctuates—and that fairly often it surges wildly upward or drops precipitously. It is true that price volatility is the most *common* characteristic of the stock market on a day-to-day basis, but it is not the most *important* characteristic. *Although stocks do swing widely in price at times, their trend is what counts: in the long run, every stock's price rises just about in direct proportion to the growth of the company's earnings and dividends.* In watching the day-to-day gyrations of stock

STANDARD & POOR'S COMPOSITE INDEX (SPZ.I)

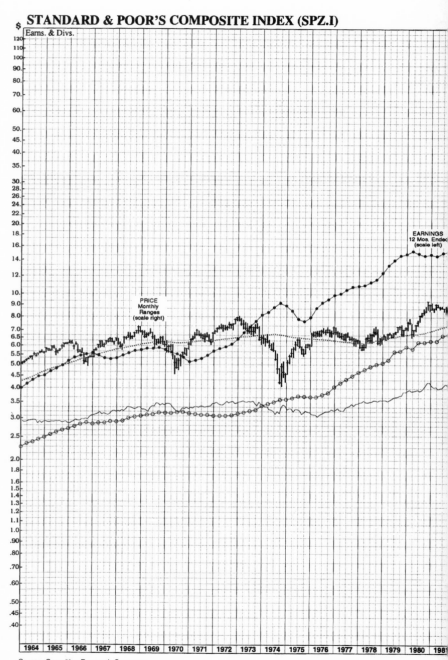

Source: Securities Research Company

10

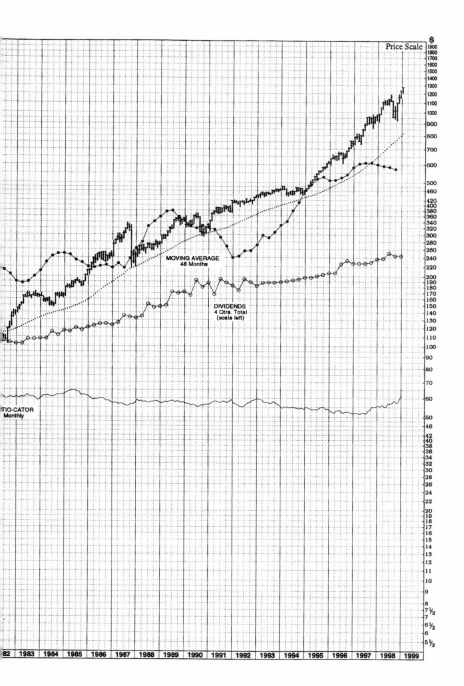

Price Scale $

MOVING AVERAGE
48 Months

DIVIDENDS
4 Qtrs. Total
(scale left)

TIO-CATOR
Monthly

1900
1800
1700
1600
1500
1400
1300
1200
1100
1000
900
800
700
600
500
460
420
400
380
360
340
320
300
280
260
240
220
200
190
180
170
160
150
140
130
120
110
100
90
80
70
60
50
46
42
40
38
36
34
32
30
28
26
24
22
20
19
18
17
16
15
14
13
12
11
10
9
8
7½
7
6½
6
5½

82 | 1983 | 1984 | 1985 | 1986 | 1987 | 1988 | 1989 | 1990 | 1991 | 1992 | 1993 | 1994 | 1995 | 1996 | 1997 | 1998 | 1999

11

prices, too often investors overlook this simple fact: most businesses steadily increase in real value as they boost their profits and their dividends to shareholders.

The S&P 500

This principle is illustrated in the chart on pages 10 and 11, which shows a thirty-five-year chart of the Standard & Poor's Composite index covering 500 large and medium-sized companies. The S&P 500 is a good measure of the performance of investment-grade stocks. In fact, it is really a better measure of the market than the more widely used Dow Jones Industrial Average, which consists of only thirty stocks.

The vertical bars on the chart represent the monthly price ranges for the S&P, the connected line of solid dots indicates earnings per share, and the connected line of circles traces dividends. Examining this chart will show you clearly two of the most important facts related to investing: *first, the long-term trend of earnings and dividends for major companies is strongly upward— not in a straight line, but nevertheless tending usually to rise; second, in the long run, stock prices advance in very close sync with earnings and dividend growth.*

Changes in the pace of profit growth and occasional periods of earnings declines usually result from variations in economic conditions, but over the thirty-five years covered by this chart, average annual growth in the S&P's earnings has been 7.4 percent. And as indicated by the close proximity of the earnings and price lines at the beginning and at the end of this long period (and quite frequently along the way), the average price of the stocks in this index has appreciated at 7.3 percent annually. That's just about a perfect correlation.

The earnings growth of these companies, which mirror the total U.S. corporate picture, has been driven by three factors: labor force growth of 1.8 percent annually, productivity gains averaging 2.0 percent, and yearly inflation of 4.4 percent, for a total of 8.2 percent. About three quarters of inflation has filtered through to profits, on top of the "real" growth forces. However, the process of filtering through was slow during the sharp rise of inflation between 1965 and 1982 and this caused earnings growth on the S&P 500 to decline to 5 percent during those years. In the "makeup" period since 1982 (when inflation slowed markedly), the S&P's earnings have risen at 8.5 percent annually. These variations in earnings growth explain why the stock market made little net progress between 1966 and 1982 and then surged ahead in the next sixteen years.

So it is basic economic forces that explain why profits grow at about 7 percent annually, and that means that the *inherent value* of the average company rises at a 7 percent pace—even though stock prices sometimes run ahead of earnings for a while when investors get more enthusiastic or lag behind earnings temporarily when the mood shifts toward pessimism. *In the long run, the market as a whole cannot outpace that basic 7 percent rate of earnings growth.*

Going way back to the mid-1920s—to include many years when inflation was under 2 percent and sometimes zero—earnings growth has averaged 6 percent annually. That's why the total return on large company stocks, as later described in Chapter 17, has averaged 11 percent per year, including 6 percent from market appreciation. The other 5 percent has come from dividends and the benefit of reinvesting that income.

Since the mid-1960s, higher inflation has added one percentage point to earnings growth, and lower dividend payout ratios (the proportion of earnings paid to shareholders) have lessened the impact of dividends on total returns. Thus, earnings growth is currently the crucial factor.

Clearly, then, earnings are the engine of the stock market.

Earnings Patterns

Broadly speaking, the long-term earnings patterns of companies fall into three categories: growth, cyclical, and stable. And generally, stock prices in each category follow similar tracks. Some examples:

GROWTH COMPANIES

First, let's look at a typical growth company: Abbott Laboratories, a very successful producer of prescription drugs, diagnostic products, intravenous solutions, nutritionals, and other hospital products. As shown in the chart on pages 16 and 17, Abbott has achieved a strong uptrend in earnings and dividends and its stock price has moved in close parallel to this growth.

Abbott's annual earnings growth since 1975 has averaged 18 percent, well over double the 7 percent growth in the S&P's earnings. However, despite the company's rapid, consistent growth in the past twenty-three years, there have been many times when its stock price dropped sharply. In fact, there were six declines of more than 25 percent, one about every three and a half years. Half of these slumps came during general bear markets, when overall investor

ABBOTT LABORATORIES (ABT)

Pharmaceuticals, hospital and laboratory products, consumer goods

$ Earns. & Divs.

M & R Dietetic Labs merged 2/28/64
Faultless Rubber acquired 10/31/66
Sorenson R acquired 10

PRICE Monthly Ranges (scale right)

Paid $.006   Paid $.008   Paid $.008   Paid $.008   Paid $.008

Adj. for 3 for 1 5/12/64

EARNINGS 12 Mos. Ended (scale left)

Paid $.002

Adj. for 2 for 1 8/25/75

Adj. for 2 for 1 5/23/78

Adj. 2 6

VOLUME-Monthly

1964 1965 1966 1967 1968 1969 1970 1971 1972 1973 1974 1975 1976 1977 1978 1979 1980

Source: Securities Research Company

16

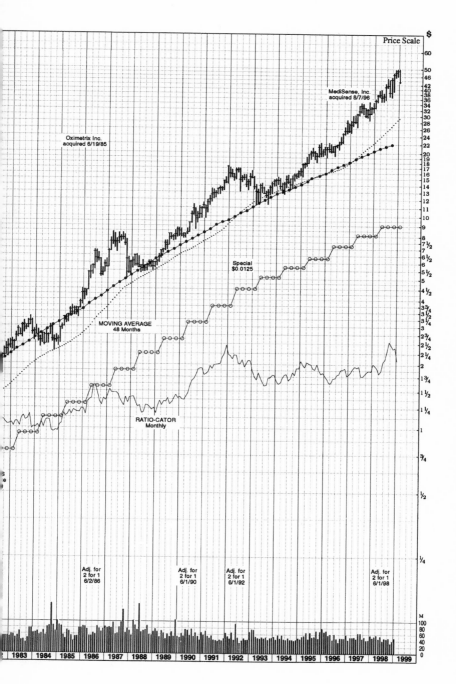

Price Scale

MediSense, Inc.
acquired 8/7/96

Oximetrix Inc.
acquired 6/19/85

Special
$0.0125

MOVING AVERAGE
48 Months

RATIO-CATOR
Monthly

$

-60
-50
-46
-42
-40
-38
-36
-34
-32
-30
-28
-26
-24
-22
-20
-19
-18
-17
-16
-15
-14
-13
-12
-11
-10
-9
-8
-7½
-7
-6½
-6
-5½
-5
-4½
-4
-3¾
-3½
-3¼
-3
-2¾
-2½
-2¼
-2
-1¾
-1½
-1¼
-1

-¾

-½

-¼

Adj. for
2 for 1
6/2/86

Adj. for
2 for 1
6/1/90

Adj. for
2 for 1
6/1/92

Adj. for
2 for 1
6/1/98

M
100
80
60
40
20
0

| 1983 | 1984 | 1985 | 1986 | 1987 | 1988 | 1989 | 1990 | 1991 | 1992 | 1993 | 1994 | 1995 | 1996 | 1997 | 1998 | 1999 |

17

attitude turned negative. The other three came when enthusiasm for health care stocks generally, or Abbott's in particular, cooled off for some temporary reason.

But as the chart illustrates dramatically, these price declines have been small ripples on a big ocean, and over the long term this stock has appreciated at slightly over 19 percent annually, very close to the company's 18 percent earnings growth.

Abbott is a classic growth company, similar to a number of other pharmaceutical manufacturers and companies like Coca-Cola, Gillette, Hewlett-Packard, and so on. Each of these companies has grown rapidly for many decades. On the other hand, there is a greater number of "temporary growth companies," ones that have expanded rapidly to become big companies over a decade or so (like Polaroid and Xerox) but then lost their momentum due to technological changes, development of new competition, or deterioration of management.

In recent years, a number of technology companies have mushroomed to a huge size—like Intel and Microsoft. But despite their current formidable strengths, it remains to be seen whether they can sustain rapid growth indefinitely. Doing so is particularly difficult in the electronics field because most types of technology change and advance rapidly, making product obsolescence high. Also, skilled people and capital (that is, venture capital) are particularly mobile in this field, so the mortality rate among technological companies is greater than in any other investment sector. For example, more than half of the original manufacturers of personal computers, disk drives, and dynamic random access memory chips (DRAMs) have disappeared in the past fifteen years.

Even that master of the technology universe, Bill Gates, recognizes those risks for his seemingly impregnable company. Speaking in mid-1998, he said, "I know very well that in the next ten years, if Microsoft is still a leader, we will have had to weather at least three crises."

CYCLICAL COMPANIES

Investing successfully in growth companies is not as easy as it looks, but it is even harder to do well in cyclical companies. General Motors (GM) is the epitome of a cyclical firm, because the demand for automobiles fluctuates widely, depending on the ability of consumers, under varying economic conditions, to purchase a product that represents a huge chunk of their annual income.

The chart on pages 20 and 21 shows the wide swings in GM's earnings since the mid-1970s, including two periods during which

★GENERAL MOTORS CORPORATION (GM)

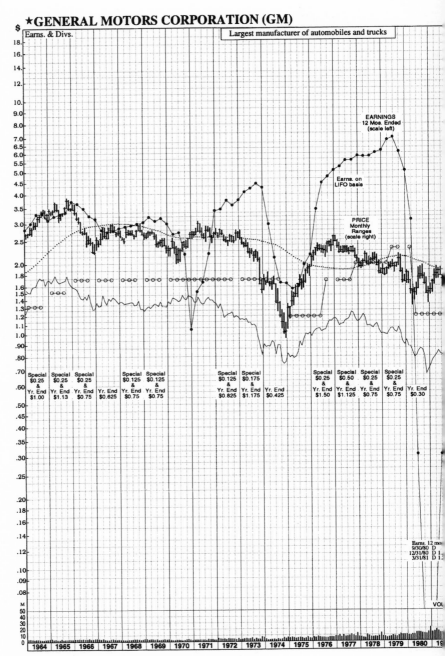

Earns. & Divs.

Largest manufacturer of automobiles and trucks

EARNINGS
12 Mos. Ended
(scale left)

Earns. on
LIFO basis

PRICE
Monthly
Ranges
(scale right)

| Special $0.25 & Yr. End $1.00 | Special $0.25 & Yr. End $1.13 | Special $0.25 & Yr. End $0.75 | Yr. End $0.625 | Special $0.125 & Yr. End $0.75 | Special $0.125 & Yr. End $0.75 | Special $0.125 & Yr. End $0.825 | Special $0.175 & Yr. End $1.175 | Yr. End $0.425 | Special $0.25 & Yr. End $1.50 | Special $0.50 & Yr. End $1.125 | Special $0.25 & Yr. End $0.75 | Special $0.25 & Yr. End $0.75 | Yr. End $0.30 |

Earns. 12 mo
9/30/80 D
12/31/80 D 1.
3/31/81 D 1.

VOL

1964 | 1965 | 1966 | 1967 | 1968 | 1969 | 1970 | 1971 | 1972 | 1973 | 1974 | 1975 | 1976 | 1977 | 1978 | 1979 | 1980 | 19

Source: Securities Research Company

20

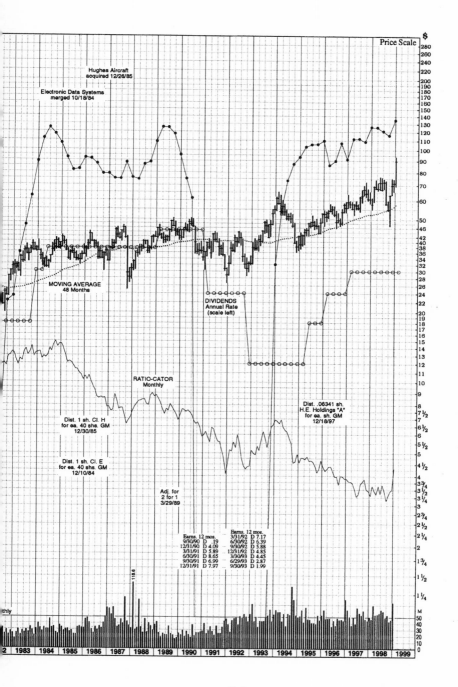

Price Scale $

Hughes Aircraft
acquired 12/26/85

Electronic Data Systems
merged 10/18/84

MOVING AVERAGE
48 Months

DIVIDENDS
Annual Rate
(scale left)

RATIO-CATOR
Monthly

Dist. .06341 sh.
H.E. Holdings "A"
for ea. sh. GM
12/18/97

Dist. 1 sh. Cl. H
for ea. 40 shs. GM
12/30/85

Dist. 1 sh. Cl. E
for ea. 40 shs. GM
12/10/84

Adj. for
2 for 1
3/29/89

118.6

Earns. 12 mos.			Earns. 12 mos.		
9/30/90	D	.19	3/31/92	D	7.17
12/31/90	D	4.09	6/30/92	D	6.39
3/31/91	D	5.89	9/30/92	D	5.88
6/30/91	D	8.65	12/31/92	D	4.85
9/30/91	D	6.99	3/30/93	D	4.45
12/31/91	D	7.97	6/29/93	D	2.87
			9/30/93	D	1.99

thly

M
50
40
30
20
10
0

1982 | 1983 | 1984 | 1985 | 1986 | 1987 | 1988 | 1989 | 1990 | 1991 | 1992 | 1993 | 1994 | 1995 | 1996 | 1997 | 1998 | 1999

21

the company ran deeply in the red. It also shows no net growth in earnings per share over several decades—because total car sales in the U.S. have grown little and GM has been losing market share.

Because GM's current earnings and dividends are no larger in the late 1990s than they were in the mid-1970s, it is not surprising that the stock has hardly risen at all over that long period, and that it has experienced lengthy price declines during periods of unfavorable earnings. Again, in the long run, stock prices do follow the trend of earnings and dividends.

STABLE COMPANIES

In contrast to the cycle-prone auto industry, the market for electric power has been rock steady, rising quite consistently at about 2 percent per year in terms of kilowatt-hours. A standout has been Duke Energy (formerly Duke Power). Operating in the favorable economic climate of North and South Carolina and benefiting from superb management, Duke has boosted its earnings and dividends at 5 percent annually since 1975. But though this is a far better record than most electric utilities, many of which have been plagued by high operating costs, problems with nuclear power plants, and regulatory difficulties, Duke's growth is still considerably slower than the 7+ percent growth rate of the S&P 500.

As can be seen from the chart on pages 24 and 25, Duke's stock has appreciated at 6.5 percent since 1975, slightly faster than earnings. This is because its margin of superiority over most other electric utilities has become increasingly evident in recent years, and Duke is quite likely to be a major winner in the competitive market for electric power and natural gas that is now developing. Nevertheless, this stock has risen at a slower rate than the market as a whole because of its slower earnings growth.

So in every company and in the market as a whole, earnings per share are like a giant magnet pulling the stock along. This magnet cannot completely overpower the major swings in investor psychology that occur periodically, but in the long run, it will determine how the stocks perform.

In considering earnings growth as the key to every stock's performance, the investor must recognize that *sustainable earnings growth* is what really counts; it determines ultimate placing in the investment marathon. Any company can boost its profits rapidly for a few quarters or even a few years by taking advantage of cyclical upswings in the economy or a temporary surge in the demand for its particular products. Aggressive

DUKE ENERGY CORPORATION (DUK)

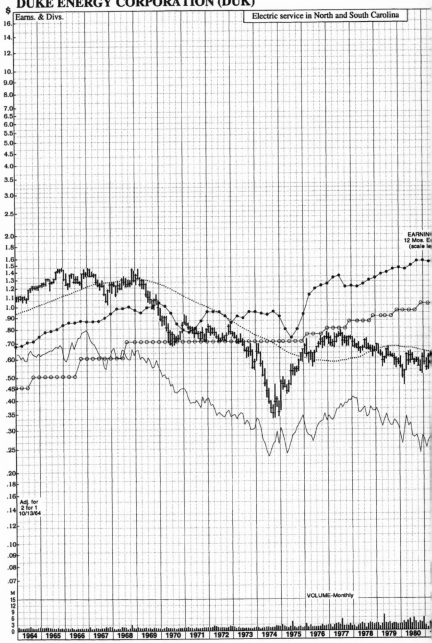

$ Earns. & Divs.

Electric service in North and South Carolina

16.
14.
12.
10.
9.0
8.0
7.0
6.5
6.0
5.5
5.0
4.5
4.0
3.5
3.0
2.5
2.0
1.8
1.6
1.5
1.4
1.3
1.2
1.1
1.0
.90
.80
.70
.60
.50
.45
.40
.35
.30
.25
.20
.18
.16
.14 Adj. for
      2 for 1
      10/13/64
.12
.10
.09
.08
.07

EARNIN
12 Mos. E
(scale le

M
15
12
9
6
3
0

VOLUME-Monthly

1964 | 1965 | 1966 | 1967 | 1968 | 1969 | 1970 | 1971 | 1972 | 1973 | 1974 | 1975 | 1976 | 1977 | 1978 | 1979 | 1980

Source: Securities Research Company

24

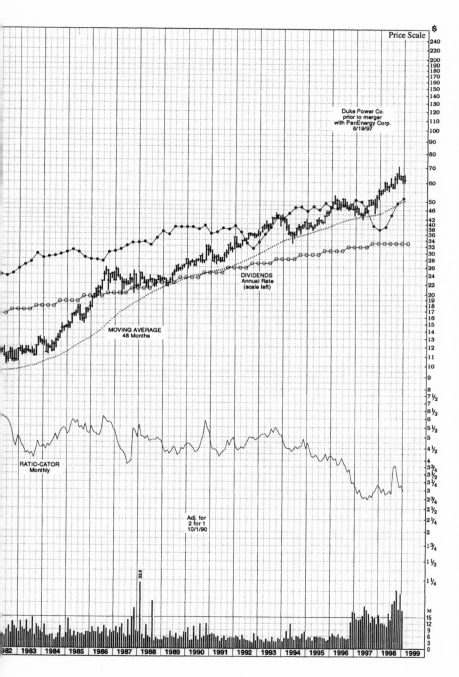

Price Scale

Duke Power Co.
prior to merger
with PanEnergy Corp.
6/19/97

DIVIDENDS
Annual Rate
(scale left)

MOVING AVERAGE
48 Months

RATIO-CATOR
Monthly

Adj. for
2 for 1
10/1/90

| 1982 | 1983 | 1984 | 1985 | 1986 | 1987 | 1988 | 1989 | 1990 | 1991 | 1992 | 1993 | 1994 | 1995 | 1996 | 1997 | 1998 | 1999 |

25

cost cutting also has an immediate benefit to earnings, but may penalize the company's long-term potential by such management actions as reducing research and development expenditures or shrinking the sales force.

For example, USX-US Steel Group doubled its earnings in the first half of 1995, and within three months its stock price jumped 35 percent. But a year later the apparent shortage of steel in the American market had ended and USX's earnings fell back to where they started, along with its stock.

Kmart was the early leader in discount retailing, but as time went on, it did not spend as much as Wal-Mart on developing sophisticated computer systems to manage inventories and buying of merchandise, or on keeping its stores attractive and up-to-date. So Wal-Mart soon caught up with Kmart; and once it passed Kmart in sales volume in 1990, Kmart's earnings stagnated for a few years and then fell some 40 percent. By 1999, Wal-Mart had run away with all the marbles, achieving sales four times those of Kmart and *profits seven and a half times greater.*

Seeing the contrast in stock performance between successful companies and underachievers leads us to the obvious question: How does the investor maximize the chances of selecting companies with strong, sustainable earnings growth?

Chapter 3

GAUGING
THE WIND

We all know it is easier to sail with the wind than against it. Yet when investors select stocks, too often they don't focus enough attention on the direction and strength of the wind in different industries. Therefore, it is very important to analyze the basic characteristics of various types of businesses and see what their *sustainable* long-term growth has been.

Past growth rates cannot be blindly projected ahead into the future, but they are a good starting point in analyzing any type of business. The following figures show thirty-five-year earnings growth rates for all the major Standard & Poor's industry groups on which there is data running back to 1960. To reinforce my point about the close correlation between earnings and dividend growth, the table on pages 28 and 29 also shows av-

Industry Groups
Annual Rates of Growth, 1963–1998

	Earnings Growth (%)	Stock Price Appreciation (%)	Appreciation as Percent of Earnings Growth
Soft Drinks	13.4	14.4	107
Drugs	12.2	13.4	110
Tobacco	12.1	13.0	107
Household Products	11.7	10.4	89
Food	9.6	10.0	104
Department Stores	9.6	9.6	100
Computer Hardware	9.3	7.0	75
Electrical Equipment	9.0	10.8	120
Machinery	7.9	7.7	97
Aerospace and Defense	7.6	9.8	129
Banks	7.6	6.9	91
Railroads	7.6	8.1	107
Oil—Domestic	7.5	8.0	107
Oil—International	7.4	8.3	112

Grocery Chains	7.2	8.7	121
Standard & Poor's 500	**7.1**	**7.8**	**110**
Life Insurance*	7.0	6.9	99
Property/Casualty Insurance*	7.0	7.1	101
Chemicals	6.6	6.3	95
Building Materials	6.2	7.3	118
Aluminum	5.7	5.0	88
Forest Products and Paper	5.7	5.7	100
Telephone	5.7	5.3	93
Gas Pipelines	5.6	6.9	123
Textiles and Apparel	5.3	6.1	115
Autos	4.6	3.4	74
Airlines	3.8	4.5	118
Electric Utilities	3.5	1.8	51
Steel	1.9	0.4	21

* Earnings for life and property/casualty insurance incomplete: 1963–1973 estimated.
Sources: Securities Research Co., David L. Babson & Co.

erage annual stock appreciation over the
same three and a half decades.

These figures illustrate several important
points. First, very few industries have been
able to achieve long-term earnings growth
rates above 10 percent (only four!). Second,
in twenty of the twenty-eight groups listed,
annual price appreciation over the past
thirty-five years has been very close to earnings growth.

Three groups, whose appreciation has been
over 20 percent faster than their earnings
growth—Aerospace and Defense, Grocery
Chains, and Gas Pipelines—have been subject to many acquisitions in the mid- and late
1990s. This has created major consolidation
in those industries and boosted stock prices.

The other industry with stock prices running well ahead of earnings growth has been
Electrical Equipment. There, the largest
company (heavily weighted in the index),
General Electric, has increased its rate of
earnings growth in the 1990s and Jack
Welch's success has stimulated investors to
increase the stock's price/earnings multiple
(P/E) more than P/Es have risen on most
other stocks.

On the negative side, four sectors have
been downgraded by investors. The stock
valuations of Autos, Electric Utilities, and
Steel have been affected by disappointing

growth. Computer Hardware has experienced a difficult transition from mainframes and minicomputers to personal computers (PCs), and throughout their existence personal computers have been subject to intense competition, holding down profit margins. So investors have downgraded the valuation of an industry that once was considered the very best.

That few industries have been able to achieve earnings growth rates and stock price rises better than 10 percent annually over the long haul explains why so few investment portfolios have been able to appreciate at double-digit rates for extended periods of time, despite their managers' best efforts to be nimble and always concentrated in the fastest-growing businesses of the moment.

What often happens with investors seeking the highest growth rates is that the stocks they own of rapidly growing companies become very popular and overpriced. Then, before portfolio managers realize that a slower pace of growth in these companies has arrived—as it usually does—their stocks have already fallen sharply, eroding much of their earlier gains. This is what happened to the big chemical stocks in the mid-1970s and the mainframe computer group stocks in the late 1980s.

Growth Factors

The particular growth trends in different industries depend on a variety of factors. Most important, obviously, is how rapidly the demand for their products and services is expanding. Often this is determined by the age and "maturity" of an industry or its ability to develop attractive new products and services.

It's hard to believe now, but in the first half of the twentieth century the production of electric power was a true growth industry. As more and more types of electrical equipment were developed and the standard of living rose, electricity sales expanded 50 to 100 percent faster than real gross domestic product (GDP). Moreover, improving technology and the development of larger-scale power plants kept reducing the cost of generating electricity, so declining kilowatt-hour prices further expanded the market for power.

But by 1960, most homes had a full complement of electric appliances and most factories and office buildings were using electric power to the maximum extent possible. So the industry reached maturity and has since grown at less than real GDP as rising power costs (stemming from higher fuel costs) have stimulated conservation.

The same pattern shows up in plastics, one of the great growth areas in the first two decades after World War II. As these synthetic materials replaced natural materials like steel, paper, and glass, they, too, gradually saturated their potential markets. For some time now the only really profitable growth in plastics has come in specialized materials, such as Lexan and other "high-performance" plastics produced by companies like General Electric.

That example illustrates the importance of research and development. Even in broad markets where demand growth is slow, the company that can come up with unique products or less costly manufacturing techniques will be able to achieve favorable sales and earnings growth.

Another example is paper, one of the oldest manufactured products in the world (first produced in China 1900 years ago). Consumption of paper in the U.S. has been growing at only 2.5 percent annually during the past fifteen years. However, in that sluggish market, a relatively small company called Albany International has prospered by making better "paper machine clothing," the continuous belts used to extract water from the slurry of pulp, chemicals, and fillers that is fed into paper-making machines at the start of the manufacturing process. Because of its superior product, Albany International has a growing business that has tripled its profits in the past decade for a 12 percent annual growth rate while the average paper company has boosted its earnings only 40 percent, for a 3.5 percent annual rate.

Similarly, a few companies like Nucor have prospered in the no-growth steel industry by developing highly efficient minimills. These turn scrap iron and steel into finished steel products that are at least as high in quality and much lower in cost than those produced by the big, expensive-to-operate traditional steel mills.

In furniture, another very old and slow-growing industry, Leggett & Platt has done well by specializing in the production of steel springs and metal frames for upholstered furniture and bedding. And Herman Miller has achieved good success by designing innovative furniture systems for offices and offering "furniture management systems" to businesses that include space design, installation, and maintenance.

But these are truly exceptions. It is difficult to become a successful niche player in a large, mature market, and there are many more good investment opportunities in industries where the basic growth in demand for the product or service is rapid.

As pointed out earlier, that growth is often sparked by research and development. For example, research and development (R&D)

plays a dominant role in the pharmaceutical business, where the aging population is providing a steadily larger customer base and advances in the biological sciences are creating many useful new products.

In the same way, the rapid advance of electronic technology is generating many growth markets in computer hardware and software—for example, in telecommunications and factory automation. As noted in the previous chapter, however, competition is intense in the technology field and the odds of a particular company achieving long-term success are surprisingly low. More often than not, today's winner is tomorrow's loser. One only has to look at Wang Laboratories, Digital Equipment, and Apple Computer to see how swiftly a great innovator and true market leader can get passed by in the technology field.

In most consumer products—beverages, food, and household products such as soaps, detergents, and toothpaste—total demand growth is not really rapid. However, the leading companies in those businesses have achieved excellent earnings growth as the table on pages 28 and 29 shows. The reasons are the great benefit of economies of scale in consumer products—which supports the huge advertising programs and distribution systems required to be efficient—and the rewards of establishing strong brand identities that allow some premium in pricing.

Despite all the taste tests claiming superiority for Coca-Cola and Pepsi Cola, those two drinks do not taste much different from the private brands sold in supermarkets and discount stores—but Coke and Pepsi have developed a superior image for their products through massive and effective advertising that persuades literally billions of customers around the world to buy their sodas. Likewise, Tide isn't really better than dozens of other laundry detergents, but Procter & Gamble has marketed it with great effectiveness. The same can be said of Lay's potato chips (part of PepsiCo) and a great majority of other branded products we buy regularly.

So the investment attractiveness of these consumer products fields is not the overall growth of the industries, which is relatively slow because there is a limit to how much we can eat and drink or how many times we have to wash our clothes. Instead, the investment appeal is based on the ability of the large companies to grow through superior marketing.

In addition, most of these firms operate internationally and demand for what we in the U.S. consider ordinary consumer products is growing at a fast pace in many "emerging" countries, along with living standards that are rising rapidly as economic development takes place. This includes much of Asia (despite a temporary interruption because of financial crises in the late 1990s), Latin America, and eastern Europe since the fall of communism.

Aside from the crucial aspect of market *growth* we've discussed, investors should pay attention to the *consistency* of different industries' growth. However, they should be alert to the danger of paying overly high stock prices for consistency. Paying up for growth consistency reflects a desire for the comfort provided by steadier investment performance. However, as we saw with Abbott Laboratories, which has one of the most consistent earnings growth records in the entire investment universe, even the steadiest growers can experience wide fluctuations in their stock prices. So paying really high prices for consistency can be dangerous.

But only so long as the investor has a truly *long-term* goal for his or her portfolio is it even worth tolerating the kind of earnings volatility that extra mildly cyclical companies experience to achieve good long-run growth.

Strong, well-managed firms like Air Products, Dayton Hudson, Dover Corp., duPont, Lowe's, PPG Industries, Southwest Airlines, and Sundstrand have managed to match the S&P 500 in long-term growth. This is a most creditable showing, but they are really the exception among cyclical firms. Many other very well-run cyclical companies, like Alcoa, Dow Chemical, and Georgia-Pacific, have not kept up over the years: the inherent growth in their markets has been just too slow.

Really superior growth in cyclical businesses is rare and seems to be confined to companies that focus on niche markets. Thus, among a representative group of 350 large and medium-sized firms, we find only two with fluctuating earnings that have outperformed the S&P over the past 25 years: Illinois Tool Works and Tyco.

Assessing Future Growth Potential

Because past growth trends don't necessarily indicate the future, one of the hardest jobs the investor faces is determining what the future growth rates of different industries are likely to be. This involves gathering all the available information and making subjective judgments about the future.

Even the most astute investor occasionally makes a mistake in projecting future growth rates for businesses. As an example, most people, including many professionals, did not realize until it became really obvious in 1991 that the market for mainframe computers and minicomputers had completely matured because of the development of personal computers and small, but powerful, workstations. The general view throughout IBM's long stagnation beginning in 1985 was that Big Blue's next major new product series would stimulate a speedup in demand. But it didn't happen. So in 1991–1992, when IBM's dire plight was suddenly dramatized by a total collapse of earnings and an 80 percent dividend cut, the stock plummeted 70 percent. Nor did a rejuvenation come in minicomputers, even though Kenneth Olsen, the founder of Digital Equipment, derided the PC as "just a toy." Some toy!

However, missing a long-term growth forecast occasionally is not fatal. As in baseball, to be successful one does not have to get a hit every time at bat. It's the *average* of the investor's decisions that determines success.

In addition to industry growth, the other essential to consider in analyzing different industries is the degree of competition and the average level of *profitability* in the business.

One rapidly growing industry that has been generally unrewarding for investors is airlines. Over the years, as anyone who struggles through today's crowded airports knows, passenger traffic has grown rapidly—in fact, at twice the rate of the overall

economy. However, in the thirty years since
the industry was deregulated it has been
brutally competitive, with almost constant
fare wars.

As a result, airline earnings have been
highly volatile, growing at only 4 percent
annually over the past thirty years. Moreover, the dividends paid by the major airlines in the late 1990s were *90 percent below
their level in the mid-1960s.* Given that
sorry record, it's remarkable that the airlines' stocks actually appreciated at an average annual rate of 3 percent. (This is why
the top airlines analyst on Wall Street told
me, "In no way are these stocks investments. They're just trading vehicles for
thrill-seekers.")

The airlines industry is so competitive because there is little or no differentiation between the services offered by various
airlines. They all have the same kind of
planes, the same kind of personnel, the
same kind of baggage service, and—unfortunately—the same kind of food.

So industry characteristics are crucial,
with huge differences between the good and
the bad. As Gerald Loeb said many years
ago, "A policy of avoidance will repay the investor many times over." In other words, it's
sensible to sail with the wind, not against it
in mediocre or poor industries.

Chapter 4

PICKING
THE BEST

Having found attractive industries to invest in, or particular sectors within industries, your next step is to determine which companies are best to buy. Again, the process should be simple and straightforward. The first thing to analyze in any company is its *competitive position*. This is determined by many factors, some of which tend to be different in different types of industries. Certainly low costs are important, whether one sells products or services, but in today's highly competitive business environment, where most companies have made great strides in improving efficiency and cutting costs, being a low-cost supplier is not enough for competitive success.

The real leaders have other attributes as well: first and foremost, superior products or services (often the result of superior re-

search and development); close customer relations and a good understanding of customer needs; excellent marketing; highly
efficient distribution (a critical factor for
suppliers to Wal-Mart); and a corporate cul-
ture that thrives on competition—as illustrated by the belief of Intel's chairman, Andy
Grove, that "only the paranoid survive."

Overarching all of these elements of success, of course, is strong management. Because most investors have little or no
opportunity to meet senior management
personnel face to face and get to know them,
we usually must judge managements by
their achievements. You can do this effectively if you study a company in detail.

Some firms have a long tradition of outstanding management—including General
Electric, Emerson Electric, Merck, Pfizer,
Coca-Cola, Intel, Hewlett-Packard, Royal
Dutch Petroleum, Schlumberger, American
International Group, and Duke Energy.
These companies have had a series of outstanding *leaders,* not just competent day-to-
day *managers;* but even some of these have
had one chief executive officer along the way
who was not up to their usual superlative
standards. When that happened, the investment community's confidence slumped for a
while and the performance of the stock suf-

fered, even though the company's health did not deteriorate greatly.

One of the most difficult challenges for investors is to appraise the new senior management of a company that has not been well run in the past. Recent success stories include Chrysler, where Lee Iacocca engineered a turnaround during the 1980s and then, after a rocky transition, Robert Eaton and Robert Lutz led the company to further success in the 1990s. Similarly, Lawrence Bossidy's move from General Electric to Allied Signal dramatically upgraded the latter's management. On the other hand, as we'll discuss in the next chapter, new managements often turn out *not* to be white knights, so many companies that have been poorly managed over long periods tend to remain mediocre or weak competitors.

A position of true leadership in a particular business is very valuable because success tends to breed even more success. Having a large market share means a company has more "muscle" and lower costs. In consumer markets, strong leadership also means stronger customer acceptance, which tends to persist.

Not all market leaders are giant corporations. In fact, many companies with strong competitive positions are leaders in small markets, or in niches within big markets, such as Albany International and Leggett & Platt, mentioned earlier; RPM, a leader in specialized paints and coatings; Sigma-Aldrich, the dominant supplier of specialty chemicals for research laboratories; Linear Technology, the leading producer of analog semiconductor chips; and Sonoco Products, a specialty packaging manufacturer.

Not every stock in a good investment portfolio has to be that of an industry leader, but the risk/reward ratio of owning any company that does not have a relatively strong competitive position in its principal markets is usually unfavorable. In business, the rich companies tend to get richer—and while the poor ones may not get poorer, they usually stay poor.

PART III

GAINING
ADVANTAGES

Chapter 5

IN OR OUT
OF THE GROOVE

Golfers and baseball players often talk about being "in the groove," having their swing follow the particular pattern that has been successful for them. Different businesses also have a "groove," a mode of performance that is typical for them, and individual stocks tend to have a normal valuation groove. However, athletes, businesses, and stocks deviate from their typical performance from time to time, doing better or worse for a while. Such periods obviously are very significant to both sports fans and investors.

Because of aging and its associated frailties, golfers and ballplayers don't always get back into the groove. However, primarily because of competitive forces, businesses and stocks usually do. Statisticians call this "regressing to the mean." Understanding this process and observing it carefully can be very rewarding—especially for those who understand the advantages of truly objective analysis and of acting at appropriate times against the prevailing consensus of investors.

Buying a high-grade stock when the company behind it is out of the groove on the negative side can often be extremely profitable. Similarly, when a company is doing better than usual in its growth and profitability, selling at least some of its shares can be advantageous, because the company is likely to slip back into its normal groove.

Most types of businesses are influenced by specific factors that give them distinctive characteristics, and all the companies in those particular businesses tend to perform in somewhat similar fashion. When one doesn't, history shows that eventually the "outlier" usually falls back in line with the industry pattern.

Banking is a good example. Traditionally, this has been a very homogeneous business. All banks deal primarily with money; it is a commodity because one bank's money is just the same as another's. They all gather deposits, primarily from individuals and businesses, and lend those funds to other individuals and businesses. They also provide financial services that are quite similar, such as cash management, custody of securities, and bill paying.

Some banks are managed better than others, so they operate a little more effectively. But in the long run, there have been few major differences in performance in this homogeneous, competitive industry—especially within geographic areas where economic conditions are similar. When a particular bank has been growing faster than its competitors, it has usually been more aggressive in lending. Eventually that will lead to greater loan losses and a slowdown of its rapid growth. Some banks have gone bonkers on loan expansion, deviating so far from the industry's normal growth pattern that they have gotten into deep trouble and even gone belly-up. So the hare loses out to the tortoise.

Continental Illinois was an early example of this phenomenon, and Bank of New England followed the same pattern a few years later. Note from the following figures that during the late 1970s–early 1980s Continental grew much more rapidly than its primary Chicago competitor, First Chicago, and another typical Midwest bank, National Bank of Detroit (NBD).

	CONTINENTAL ILLINOIS	FIRST CHICAGO	NBD
Loan Growth 1977–1983	104%	71%	56%
Stock Price 12/31/77	26	18½	6
9/30/90	0	17	25

In the late 1970s and early 1980s Continental was widely admired for its "excellent growth," but then it became apparent that the bank's rapid expansion had been fueled mainly by making risky loans in the oil patch, which was outside its territory and area of competence. It was lending lots of money to customers that banks who knew the oil industry well considered too risky at a time when oil prices had more than doubled. Continental's bubble burst as fast as the oil price bubble did in the mid-1980s, and its demise in 1989 points up the perils of trying to grow much faster than the fundamental trends in your business. Meanwhile, First Chicago chugged along in good shape, while National Bank of Detroit, its lending policies tempered by long experience with the ups and downs of the auto industry, did extremely well. The net result was a wide disparity in stock performance.

In a later example, Bank of New England was super-aggressive in expanding during the mid-1980s, both internally and through acquisitions. While its record looked good for quite a while, the sheer pace of such growth (primarily in the real estate market during that boom) turned out to be unmanageable and the chickens of risky loans then came home to roost. So Bank of New England also went down the drain while its more carefully managed neighbor, BayBanks, survived the difficulties of the late 1980s extremely well and went on to prosper mightily up to the time of its merger with BankBoston in 1997.

	BANK OF NEW ENGLAND	BAYBANKS
Growth 1982–1988		
Number of Offices	87%*	13%
Loan Volume	347*	263
Stock Price 12/31/82	13	15
9/30/90	0	14

* Combined growth for Connecticut Bank & Trust and original Bank of New England, which merged in 1985.

On the other side of the coin, growing more slowly than your industry is usually frowned on by investors. However, it offers great potential rewards when, as occasionally occurs in this era of increased shareholder activism, the existing management or a new one gets the company back in the groove. This is what happened to CPC (the

food company that later split into Best
Foods and Corn Products International in
1997) when a corporate raider tried to take
over the company in the late 1980s.

As the following table shows, CPC's earnings had been growing much more slowly
than those of the overall food industry from
1977 to 1987. But once management woke
up and started running the business more
effectively, the company's profit gains accelerated, while growth for the rest of the industry slowed down as competition
intensified in many types of packaged food.
So while CPC got back into its old groove,
most of its competitors fell temporarily
below their former pace.

	CPC	FOOD INDUSTRY*
Annual Growth 1977–1987		
Earnings per Share	7.2%	12.7%
Annual Growth 1987–1997		
Earnings per Share	9.4	5.0
Stock Price		
12/31/77	6	3
12/31/87	20	14
12/31/97	109	49
1977–1987 Appreciation	+233%	+366%
1987–1997 Appreciation	+445	+250

* S&P Food Index.

Just as most businesses have typical *growth* patterns that are hard to deviate from, different industries and individual companies within them also have different *profitability* norms. These are set primarily by the basic economics of the business—especially by its competitive nature. When a company's profitability moves above or below its long-term norm, the impact on its stock can be substantial. For example, the old Westinghouse Electric Corporation (which evolved into CBS in 1997 after divesting all its manufacturing operations) achieved what for it was unusually high profitability during the 1980s. Primarily because it successfully entered real estate development, a business far removed from electrical equipment, the company's return on equity capital rose well above previous levels in the teens to reach a peak of 26 percent in 1990. As a result, its stock appreciated sevenfold during that decade, while the market as a whole merely tripled. But then the real estate bubble burst and the profitability of the rest of Westinghouse's businesses could only roll along at the old mid-teens rate, so operating earnings fell 85 percent and the stock followed suit.

Colgate's experience in the early 1980s illustrates the reverse side of the coin. After being very good for many years, the company's performance deteriorated markedly in 1980–1981 and stayed sluggish through 1985. So earnings went flat after two decades of consistently growing at 9 percent annually—and return on equity, which had been running over 20 percent, fell to the low teens. As usually happens, this stimulated several key management changes over several years and Colgate then began to exploit its inherent strengths. Operating performance improved until it was better than ever. Since 1985, Colgate's earnings growth has accelerated to 13 percent annually as sales gained momentum and return on equity rose to 30 percent. This made the stock a big winner in the 1990s.

Many investors do not understand the powerful forces that usually cause companies' performance to regress to their mean. They then get trapped in cyclical stocks that are in a periodic, but temporary, positive phase.

The paper industry is a good example. The fundamental factors in the paper industry are not favorable. Growth in demand for paper products is extremely slow and paper factories represent a huge investment, so there is great incentive for manufacturers to run their plants at high rates all the time. When demand is strong, paper prices rise and company profits soar, but when demand slackens, the manufacturers cut prices to try to attract enough business to keep their mills operating at full capacity. This doesn't work, because every company is attempting to do the same thing.

Few industries have greater swings in profitability than paper, as shown in the following table.

	S&P PAPER AND FOREST PRODUCTS GROUP		S&P 500	
	EARNINGS	STOCK PRICE	EARNINGS	STOCK PRICE
1982 Low	$0.47	6	$12.65	102
1989 High	3.10	26	22.87	360
1992 Low	0.73	21	19.09	395
1995 High	3.90	37	33.96	622
1997 Low	0.93	29	45.20	970
Cumulative Growth	98%	383%	257%	850%

In each paper industry up cycle, which lasts several years or longer, investors get enthusiastic about the industry's strong profit gains and pile into the stocks near the industry's cyclical peak—because they always look cheap against the good earnings. At the 1989 high-water mark, paper stocks were selling at eight times earnings, while the S&P had a multiple of sixteen. And at the 1995 high, paper stocks were selling at nine times earnings versus eighteen for the S&P.

Of course, what investors forget is that good earnings are the exception in the paper industry, not the rule. Competitive forces always push these companies back into their groove of relatively low profitability and very slow secular (long-term) growth. These two characteristics explain why paper companies' long-term earnings gains and stock price appreciation are both much less than those of the average business.

If it were possible to time the cycles correctly, to buy at the lows and sell at the highs, one could make a lot of money in paper stocks; but history shows that few people have the courage or foresight to time such moves successfully. At best, they tend to be half a cycle behind, and trading records indicate that many investors buy near the highs and sell after the stocks have dropped sharply.

So one of the most important tasks for investors when looking at any industry or company is to determine where it is relative to its norm or groove. This requires taking a long-term perspective, which has been increasingly difficult to do as the market has become more and more oriented toward the short term.

Just as the forces of long-term growth can be powerful, so can those factors that tend to push any company to perform in line with its particular norm. Understanding these characteristics can help you make wise investment decisions. So here are three simple tests that can be used to make intelligent stock purchases and sales. All are based on what is actually going on in a business.

First, is the business growing more rapidly or slowly than the typical pattern for that company and its industry?

Second, is the company's profit margin above or below its historical norm?

Third, is the current superior or inferior performance of the company reflected in an historically high or low valuation for the stock?

Because company performance almost always tends to regress to the mean, a stock is probably a good buy when growth and/or profitability is below the company's norm. When the company's performance is out of its groove on the high side, its stock is probably vulnerable.

The reason this simple rule generally applies is that most investors take a relatively short-term view and, as noted earlier, assume that what has happened recently will continue. They fail to recognize that economic and market forces are always working to press companies and entire industries back toward their respective grooves.

Determining whether a company is above, below, or in line with its growth and profitability norms is usually quite easy. Doing such an analysis can keep you from being trapped by the consensus of the moment—and that's the single factor that causes more mistakes by most investors than any other.

The Rare Long-Term Underachiever

A final comment on regressing to the mean: occasionally a hitherto good company does not get back into its groove after it has begun to underperform its past norms. In rare instances, a problem develops that really cripples a firm, like the difficulties with asbestos that wiped out Johns-Manville.

Also, there are instances of very strong companies falling into a rut caused by changing industry conditions and poor management, and staying mired for many years. This happened to Sears Roebuck after it began to encounter intense competition from discounters in the early 1970s. It wasn't until the late 1990s that Sears began to show signs of successful redirection.

Eastman Kodak is another old blue-chip company that started to lose its momentum in the 1970s, and even with a strong new management team in the late 1990s, it is far from getting back into its old groove. Complacency about its past success left Kodak ill prepared to cope with the advent of extremely strong competition from Fuji. And now Kodak also faces the potential threat of electronic photography, which will have many more participants and much lower profit margins than chemical film.

Chapter 6

HOW SKEPTICISM PAYS

Investors should repeat to themselves over and over again that when something looks too good to be true, it probably is. This old adage is a real gem of investment wisdom. As I look back over my decades of experience, I find that the most frequent cause of my mistakes has been accepting the market consensus—sometimes overly positive, sometimes far too negative—when a skeptical, independent analysis would have produced a much more realistic judgment. The message for investors is: *be a sensible skeptic.*

Following the herd leads people into far more trouble than any other error they make with stocks. It is difficult to avoid getting caught up in the popular enthusiasms and pessimisms of the moment, so people tend to buy stocks when they're popular and sell them when they're unpopular. The pattern of drug stocks in the 1990s shows this tendency clearly.

In the early part of the decade, when overall corporate profits were being held down by a recession and heavy restructuring expenses, the earnings of leading pharmaceutical manufacturers actually accelerated to a 17 percent annual growth rate from the industry's historical rate of 10 percent. This speedup in a period of general slowdown caused drug stocks to rise much faster than the overall market. From the end of 1989 to the beginning of 1992, pharmaceutical shares jumped 80 percent while the overall market rose just 18 percent.

That happened because everything about the drug business looked fabulous. The companies were bringing out many exciting new products and putting high prices on them, and they were raising prices of older drugs at nearly twice the rate of inflation. Naturally, this boosted profit margins dramatically, helping to push the price/earnings ratio on the average drug stock up from 15 to 25 in just 24 months.

However, the skeptic who took a hard look at the pharmaceutical industry in 1992 would have seen several things to be concerned about.

First, unit sales of drugs were growing at only 2 to 3 percent per year, so most of the industry's strong revenue growth was coming from price increases. Second, health care costs in the United States were rising extremely rapidly, creating a heavy expense burden for consumers, their employers, and the government. At the same time, the number of people enrolling in health maintenance organizations and other forms of managed care programs was starting to grow rapidly, tending to concentrate drug purchase decisions in the hands of large, sophisticated buyers.

So pressures were mounting on the key source of the industry's recent rapid profit growth: price increases. The diligent skeptic would have concluded that while this was still a good industry, it had not become *better* in terms of its fundamental characteristics, and the acceleration of earnings growth since the late 1980s could well prove to be a temporary phenomenon.

Of course, drug pricing did become a major issue in Washington, and one of the key thrusts of the complex program to totally revamp health care delivery, designed by Hillary Clinton and members of her husband's administration, included severe limits on drug prices. This really scared enthusiasts for drug stocks, so from their peaks in January 1992 to their lows in July 1993 those companies' shares dropped an average of 35 percent while the market as a whole remained essentially flat.

But this conventional wisdom was also wrong.

Only the skeptics were pointing out in 1993–1994, when the stocks hit new lows, that pharmaceutical manufacturers were continuing to develop excellent new drugs whose much-needed therapies would provide large additional sales and favorable profit opportunities, even in an environment of limited price increases on older pharmaceuticals.

These independent thinkers also cited the rapid aging of the population that should soon start to boost unit sales of prescription drugs—as well as the fact that advances in pharmaceutical development were making those products much more cost effective for treating certain diseases than hospitalization and surgery.

All these factors did come into play in the next few years. Meanwhile, the overbearing, harsh Clinton health plan was soon torpedoed in the early stages of Congressional hearings. However, while prescription drug price increases did slow markedly, the industry embarked on another strong phase of growth and in 1994–1997 drug stocks again outperformed the market by a wide margin, more than tripling in value while the overall market slightly more than doubled.

Aside from unprecedented surges in company performance, there are other factors that tend to make companies and their stocks look too good to be true. One is the constant effort by most managements to put their best foot forward in talking with analysts and other investors. In the words of the old song, most executives tend to "accentuate the positive and eliminate the negative," or at least gloss over unfavorable facts.

Even the most honest managements usually present their companies in the best possible light, although few try to dissemble as much as the CEO of a major corporation who wrote in the first paragraph of his company's 1971 annual report, "We're pleased to report another record year for your company, as our sales rose 9 percent to a new peak of $3.3 billion," and then made the reader struggle through many paragraphs to find out that net income and earnings per share had dropped 18 percent.

Although few managements are really dishonest in what they say or in the numbers their companies report, the investor should always assume that what he or she sees and hears directly from the company has some degree of positive spin on it. This is why good analysts check out every company by talking to its competitors, suppliers, and customers—to get what broadcaster Paul Harvey calls "the rest of the story."

Another source of investor excitement that has to be viewed with some skepticism is new products and services that seem to have great potential for becoming large, highly profitable businesses. A number of new products and services do, but at least an equal number do not, turning out to be temporary fads in the investment community.

Here, too, investors must make a dispassionate analysis of the product, its potential market, and the likelihood that competitors will join the fray, limiting profitability for all participants.

In this vein, it's instructive to review the many fads that generated great enthusiasm and high stock prices in the investment community over our lifetimes before sinking into oblivion.

Bowling and Boats

As the U.S. gained prosperity after the long depression of the 1930s and four years of World War II, the concept of discretionary income began to develop. Investors decided that millions of people would have enough extra income to spend on much more recreational activity. That concept was married with such technological developments as the development of automatic pinsetting machines for bowling alleys and the advent of fiberglass-reinforced plastics, which were much cheaper for boat manufacture than wood. Thus was created a boom in the stocks of bowling equipment and boat manufacturers. These actually were *the most popular stocks* in the market (except for IBM) in the late 1950s. But the markets for these products were not infinite, so when growth decelerated and competition intensified, the best of the companies in those fields saw their stocks drop 60 to 90 percent and the weaker participants went bankrupt.

Conglomerates

In the 1960s, conglomerates became all the rage. The idea of building a "portfolio of businesses" in all sorts of unrelated activities was promoted as a new way to achieve superior corporate growth and, through the advantages of diversification, to provide much more stability in operating performance. A key concept in the conglomerate theory was synergy; somehow the different activities would lend strength to each other through a mysterious process of cross-fertilization. But the skeptics asked how

Stouffer Foods and inertial guidance systems for aircraft would benefit each other under the umbrella of Litton Industries, or how Continental Baking, Scotts grass seeds, Hartford Insurance, Rayonier's pulp and paper business, and Sheraton hotels would all benefit each other in the large ITT empire (even with the guiding genius of Harold Geneen). The answers that came back from the managements were really impossible to decipher.

Even so, the conglomerates did achieve strong earnings growth for about five years, and it took the skeptics a little while to learn that *all* those gains were coming from "bootstrapping" earnings, by swapping the conglomerates' shares at price/earnings ratios of about 12 for the acquirees' stock, which had P/Es of about 7 to 8 in that low valuation era. And once it became apparent that these large and increasingly complex companies were not achieving any synergy or any internal earnings growth, their stocks dropped about 75 percent.

Protecting the Environment

In succeeding years, growing concern with protecting the environment created a fad for companies that had any role in helping to clean up the land or the air. However, government and corporate spending on the environment proved to be widely fragmented and not nearly as large as investors had expected; so environmental stocks fell from grace, producing huge losses for their owners.

Carpets and Restaurant Franchising

Then came the carpet industry, where a new manufacturing technique called tufting and new synthetic fibers greatly broadened the market and, amazingly, led the electronics giant of that day, RCA Corporation, to pay a big price for a carpet company—just as that industry became intensely competitive and saw its growth slow down. The next fad was restaurant franchising, after the early success of McDonald's. This was also followed within a few years by a big shakeout, when companies trading on the names of Grand Ol' Opry star Minnie Pearl and four prominent National Football League quarterbacks imploded.

Technology

A period of technology fads was next. Notable in its early phase was the advent of robotics and computer-aided design and computer-aided manufacturing (CAD-CAM). As long as Roger Smith, the CEO of

General Motors, thought he could replace thousands of his workers with robots, those stocks had their day in the sun. CAD-CAM was just as brief a Roman candle. It was a revolutionary technology, but like robots, its market was relatively limited. At the zenith of this fad, Computervision, the leading CAD-CAM company, had the highest price/earnings ratio on the New York Stock Exchange, nearly triple the multiple on the S&P 500. At that point, one of my firm's clients told me, "I don't care what the P/E multiple is on Computervision. CAD-CAM is the wave of the future and I've got to own the stock." Soon thereafter, the limited market for this technology became obvious and the stock went into free fall.

Investors should always be wary of "waves of the future" and "gotta-own" stocks. As we look back at these fads and wonder how they ever could have become so popular, we should heed the words of Henry David Thoreau, written in 1854: "Every generation laughs at the old fashions, but follows religiously the new."

That warning is particularly apt as the 1990s end with one of the greatest stock market manias ever: Internet companies. In that burgeoning field there will undoubtedly be a *few* long-term winners among the current favorites—but the wild passion for these embryonic companies that have little or no current earnings will produce *many* costly failures for the starry-eyed investors who are pursuing them with manic fervor.

Conventional wisdom can also be terribly wrong about the overall market, because investors are susceptible to extreme swings in emotion that generate all the force of mob psychology. The two most striking examples of this came in *Business Week,* a generally estimable publication.

The first was a cover story published in February 1969, captioned "Can the Bond Market Survive?" It concluded that, "In the long run, the public market for straight debt might become obsolete." True, the bond market did very poorly in the next dozen years, but the investor who bought long-term bonds back then enjoyed a 7 percent yield in the next thirty years. More important, "the public market for straight debt" burgeoned once inflation slackened, boosting total debt of domestic nonfinancial sectors more than twelvefold by 1998.

The second example was a cover story published on August 13, 1979, near the peak of runaway inflation and all its devastation, and after the stock market had not risen at all in sixteen years. The headline read, "The Death of Equities," and the lead paragraph said, "Today the old attitude of buying solid stocks as a cornerstone for one's life savings and retirement has simply disappeared. Says a young U.S. executive: 'Have you been to an American stockholders' meeting lately? They're all old fogies. The stock market is just not where the action's at.' " The Dow Jones Average on that day was 888. The old fogies are laughing happily today and the young executive is still trying to play catch-up.

In addition to conventional wisdom, investors should also be skeptical about the stock opinions and company earnings estimates of the big Wall Street brokerage firms' equity analysts. These firms have large investment banking operations that make huge profits from selling new issues of companies' stock to the public. So their analysts work hard to maintain friendly relations with the corporations they analyze and write so-called research reports about, in the hope of attracting investment banking business. These analysts cast their evaluations in the most favorable light possible. This bias keeps most of them from *ever* issuing a "sell" report—and even a "neutral" or "average market performer" opinion is rare from the big investment banking/brokerage firms.

Some of this bias also shows up in the consistently overoptimistic earnings forecasts of Wall Street analysts. Various studies have shown that these projections for earnings over just the short time frame of twelve months ahead are, on average, more than 10 percent above what actually happens.

For example, an analysis by Vijay Kuma Chopra, published in the November/December issue of *The Financial Analysts Journal,* showed that from 1985 through 1997, a large group of analysts' twelve-month projections for companies in the S&P 500 averaged an increase of 17.7 percent, which was more than twice the actual growth that occurred. In aggregate, the projections were 11.2 percentage points above what the companies finally reported. Such a huge margin of error (which occurs almost every year) leads investors who rely on these analysts' forecasts to make lots of costly mistakes.

Another factor feeding analysts' positive bias is their natural tendency to fall in love with their companies, aided and abetted by the positive spin that managements usually put on their businesses. Typically, analysts really get to *like* the companies they follow, and it's just plain difficult for them to be sensible skeptics.

So how do we avoid this trap of rushing along with the crowd over the edge of one cliff after another? Clearly, the answer for us is to be skeptics. Through the years, we've heard a lot about the "contrary approach" to investing. It has considerable merit, and what I am suggesting relates to the contrarian's method—but there is a difference. Webster's dictionary describes the word *contrarian* as meaning "inclined to oppose or disagree stubbornly." In investing, that can lead one to develop an opinion *just because* it runs counter to the general view.

On the other hand, the dictionary calls a *skeptic* "a person who habitually doubts, questions, or suspends judgment upon matters generally accepted." I think that's exactly what you should do as a sensible investor. You should look at the facts and interpret them with your own common sense. Frequently this will lead you to accept the conventional wisdom, but often it will tell you—very advantageously—that what most people believe to be true probably isn't.

As a skeptic, you will not only avoid the risks produced by bursts of enthusiasm, but more important, you will take advantage of the tremendous money-making opportunities that develop when the pendulum swings toward overpessimism or outright panic about an individual company or industry, or the market as a whole, by buying stocks that are irrationally disliked.

Beyond just having a generally questioning attitude, an investment skeptic should also *do the math*. That means taking every optimistic scenario for a particular company or industry and working through the numbers on likely future sales and earnings, to see whether they can produce high enough share prices in the future (at *realistic* stock valuations) to make the present prices of those shares reasonable or excessively high.

So when people in 1999 tell you that the Dow Jones Average is going to hit 20,000 by 2002, ask them what earnings growth and P/E are going to make that happen. Very likely they haven't even thought about that.

Chapter 7

MAKING DOLLARS REALLY WORK

Getting full value for all the investment dollars one has painstakingly accumulated is extremely important. That can only be done by carefully analyzing the stock market's valuation of individual companies. Valuation is the statistical measurement—one could say the objective, cold-blooded measurement—of investor enthusiasms and pessimisms about stocks. When investors are optimistic about a particular company, or the market as a whole, they pay higher prices for a dollar of earnings, dividends, and asset values. On the other hand, when they are pessimistic, they pay lower prices.

In making buy, sell, and hold decisions, after evaluating the fundamentals of a company's business, one then has to look carefully at the valuation of its stock—to

determine whether it is high, low, or some-
where in between. This is extremely important because stocks with low valuations
relative to various historical yardsticks almost always provide better returns to investors than stocks with high valuations.
    So what are the yardsticks?

Price/Earnings Ratio

The most widely used is the price/earnings
ratio: stock price divided by earnings per
share. A P/E of 10 means that it costs $10 in
the stock market to buy $1 of earnings per
share. And a multiple of 20 means the investor has to pay $20 to buy $1 of earnings.
    The price/earnings ratio is a logical yard-
stick because the worth of most businesses
depends directly on how much they earn. If
you were looking at two gas stations in your
town to determine which one you would buy,
and one generated twice as much annual
profit as the other, you would probably pay
twice as much for that station. In the stock
market, it is not quite that simple—because
investors, very logically, are willing to pay
higher price/earnings ratios for strong, established companies that are leaders in
their fields, for more rapidly growing firms,
and for those with very consistent profit
growth. These are the qualitative factors

that have to be entered into the price/earnings ratio equation.

Dividend Yield

Dividend yield is another measure of stock valuation, but it is useful primarily in comparing companies that are very similar in their type of business, rates of profitability, and growth. So the fact that a slow-growing electric utility has a dividend yield of 6 percent, while a rapidly growing computer software company has a yield of 0.5 percent, or even zero, doesn't by itself make the utility stock a better value. Dividend yield lost much of its usefulness as a valuation measure during the 1990s because companies are paying a smaller proportion of their earnings to shareholders in dividends and using sizable amounts of cash flow to repurchase stock, thus creating a discontinuity in yield patterns.

Price/Book Value

The other traditional valuation yardstick is price/book value ratio. Book value is the total net worth of the company—paid-in capital and retained earnings or earned surplus—divided by the number of shares outstanding. In other words, it is the total value of the company's assets as carried on its balance sheet, minus its liabilities and all its debt. The key problem with book value is that all the assets are stated at their cost less accumulated depreciation. In any sort of inflationary environment, most of those assets would have a current market value—if one were to sell them—higher than historical cost. So some analysts use price indexes to try to determine the "replacement book value"—what it would cost to replace the company's assets at today's market prices, recognizing, of course, that older assets have depreciated in real value. Estimating such replacement values is very hard. Another difficulty with book value as a valuation tool these days is the recent corporate practice of taking large write-offs during corporate restructuring (and in connection with acquisitions) and making large share repurchases. These practices have lowered book values substantially, making comparisons with past price/book ratios meaningless.

The Winner: P/E

What it comes down to is that price/earnings ratio has become, more than ever, the most effective valuation yardstick. In using it, though, we must recognize that reported earnings are far from precise. The latitude in accounting rules, and the desire of some managements to push the rules to their limit, means that some companies' earnings numbers are quite puffed up while others' are very conservatively stated. Therefore, it is always important to try to discern the "quality" of a particular company's reported earnings when assessing its valuation in the market. Obviously, one should pay a higher P/E for conservatively stated earnings than "liberal" ones—just as one should pay more for firms with higher profitability, more rapid growth, and more consistent profit performance.

Because of their differences on these factors and others, the typical market valuations of individual companies and groups of companies vary greatly. Reflecting its superiority as a business on all scores, Wal-Mart has generally sold at twice the P/E of Kmart (when Kmart has had satisfactory earnings). Similarly, Intel has usually been valued at up to twice the multiple of Advanced Micro Devices, and drug stocks have generally had P/Es three times those of auto stocks.

Typical, "normal" valuation patterns reflect pure logic—but I want to reemphasize that at times investor emotions overpower logic, driving stock valuations to extremes. The resulting extra-high or extra-low valuations may persist for considerable periods, but eventually the fundamental force of earnings reasserts itself and valuations move back toward their normal level. This is still another example of "regressing to the mean."

So price/earnings ratios really are the fever thermometer of investor emotions, and shifts in emotions are an extremely important influence on stock performance over the short and intermediate term, ranging from a few months to several years or even longer. Coca-Cola stock vividly illustrates the extreme valuation swings that even a prime, blue-chip investment can go through and how badly even an ultimately successful company's stock can perform for periods of many years after becoming overvalued.

COCA-COLA: HIGHS AND LOWS IN P/E

1973	45	1992	33
1982	8	1994	20
1986	23	1998	55
1988	14		

COCA-COLA: PRICE PERFORMANCE DURING P/E DECLINES

	COCA-COLA	S&P 500	COCA-COLA vs. S&P
1973–1982	−60%	−3%	−57%
1986–1987	−25	+21	−46
1992–1994	−15	+7	−22

There are two ways to use the P/E yardstick in measuring stock valuations. First is the stock's current multiple versus its past range of P/Es. Second is where the stock's current multiple stands in relation to the prevailing valuation of "the market" (generally the S&P 500) and how that "P/E relative" compares with past relatives. Here's how Coca-Cola looks on those bases since it reached a peak valuation at the top of "The Two-Tier Market" in 1973, when a handful of companies, often called "The Nifty Fifty," reached extreme P/E premiums.

COCA-COLA: P/Es

	COCA-COLA P/E	P/E RELATIVE TO S&P 500
1973	45	2.5
1982	8	0.8
1986	23	1.5
1988	14	1.3
1992	33	1.8
1994	20	1.3
1998	55	1.9
36-Year Average	23	1.6

Several points stand out. First, over the nearly four decades covered, Coca-Cola's *average* P/E ratio has been 23. But after the two times prior to 1998 when its multiple rose well above that "norm" (1973 and 1992), the stock performed poorly for periods of nine years and two years, respectively. Second, *on average,* Coke's stock has sold at a P/E 60 percent higher than that of the average 500 companies in the S&P Composite Index. But after the two years in which its P/E relative had moved well above that premium (also 1973 and 1992), the same underperformance occurred. Third, even after the stock just got back to its *average* valuation level in 1986, after many years of undervaluation, it performed poorly for two years.

It's true that, for the long-term investor, owning a stock that lags behind the market for a couple of years or even longer shouldn't be a problem as long as the stock gets back on track and outperforms the market thereafter. However, the risk is that one will get discouraged with a laggard that was purchased at a high valuation and sell it *after* it has performed poorly. I've seen this happen many times, with investors selling good stocks near their lows, just when they should have been *buying.* Another example of emotion overpowering reason.

Not surprisingly, there are great differences in *long-term* investment results between buying even an exceptional company like Coca-Cola at high valuation points and low ones.

COCA-COLA: CUMULATIVE PRICE APPRECIATION TO 1998 (9/18)

PURCHASE DATE	P/E	APPRECIATION (%)
1973 High	45	1893
1982 Low	8	4780
1986 High	23	1000
1988 Low	14	1571
1992 High	33	165
1994 Low	20	221

No matter how sophisticated one's valuation analysis, it's impossible to determine the *ideal* time to be buying or selling any stock. But successful investing does not require pinpoint accuracy, only dealing sensibly in orders of magnitude. In this case, all that's necessary is to determine general ranges of overvaluation, reasonable valuation, and undervaluation. The kind of valuation analysis I've recommended works well because, as discussed in Chapter 5, the basic characteristics of various businesses and individual companies change very slowly, if at all, over long periods of time—so their typical valuation patterns also persist.

The general level of price/earnings ratios in the market is affected by two things: the mood of investors, as we've just discussed, and the interrelated pattern of inflation and interest rates. When the economy is doing well and corporate profits are rising strongly, investors are usually optimistic and P/Es are in the upper part of their long-term range. But when business is poor and earnings are disappointing, as occurred much of the time from the mid-1970s to the early 1980s, pessimism prevails and valuations go down.

The Impact of Inflation and Interest Rates

Sometimes correlated with these ebbs and flows are the levels of inflation and interest rates. When inflation accelerates, bond investors quickly react by demanding higher yields. They want to offset the greater erosion of the purchasing power of the fixed income they get from their semiannual interest payments and the fixed amount of principal they will be paid at the maturity of their bonds. So higher inflation boosts interest rates—and higher yields on bonds make them more attractive relative to stocks. Thus, P/Es on stocks soon fall to maintain their degree of relative attraction. And the reverse happens when inflation and interest rates decline.

Two striking examples of the impact of interest rates on P/Es occurred in 1987 and 1997–1998. In October 1987, long-term interest rates began to move up toward 10 percent, the highest level in two years and almost up to the long-term total return of 10½ percent from stocks. This helped cause a quick drop in P/Es and was a major factor in the record-breaking stock market crash that month that pushed prices down 25 percent in just two trading days. On the brighter side, during 1997–1998, as inflation slowed to a thirty-year low of under 2 percent, intermediate- and long-term interest rates fell to their lowest level in nearly three decades. In response, the P/E on the S&P rose from 19 to 28, the highest valuation ever.

Predicting changes in interest rates is just as difficult as predicting upward and downward moves in the stock market. Even the most knowledgeable economists and bond market analysts have had a very poor record of forecasting rates (as will be demonstrated in Chapter 12).

So the equity investor should just "go with the flow" as far as the impact of inflation and interest rates on P/Es is concerned. Be aware of what is happening, but don't try even to guess how rates may change and thus affect the general level of P/Es. Instead, recognize that low interest rates and resulting high price/earnings ratios usually mean that general economic conditions are good, and that investor optimism has made the risk/reward ratio for stocks temporarily less favorable.

———

One specialized valuation tool deserves brief mention. Because ownership of oil and gas in the ground or proven mineral reserves represents a sure source of future earnings—unless the prices of such materials fall excessively—a key method of evaluating natural resources companies is assigning values to their reserves. This requires such knowledge as the quality of the reserves and probable extraction costs, which only experienced specialists are likely to have. And even here, the ultimate question is, how much earnings will those assets produce in the future?

Chapter 8

DON'T BE A SUCKER

Nowhere is valuation more important than in popular stocks. I've found that investors have suffered much greater losses from buying the hot favorites of the moment than from any other type of stock. It's another case of swallowing the consensus hook, line, and sinker. So don't bet on the widely recognized sure thing—the stock that looks certain to be a big winner. Even among otherwise rational people, surges of enthusiasm for the companies that are growing most rapidly at the moment tend to push the prices of those firms' stocks up to risky, and usually unsustainable, levels. The excessive optimism reflected in the prices of such shares makes it virtually impossible for these companies to meet the euphoric expectations of investors. This is why so many popular stocks turn out to be unrewarding investments and even disastrous holdings.

To demonstrate the perils of popularity, I have made a study over the past sixteen years, tracing the subsequent performance of the particular stock on the New York Stock Exchange that was most popular in the spring of each year. That stock has had the highest price/earnings ratio on the Exchange in April (just to use the same month consistently each year) and typically its multiple has been about triple the valuation of "the market" as measured by the Standard & Poor's 500. Note how these favorites have performed as summarized in the table on pages 92 and 93.

On average, the most popular stocks appreciated *less than half* as much as the S&P if held from their peak of popularity through to June 1998.

Moreover, if the one huge winner in the list (Cullinane, then Cullinet, whose success has come almost entirely since its acquisition by Computer Associates) were excluded, the remaining fourteen companies' shares have appreciated just *one sixth* as much as the S&P over the various time periods. This is because only four of the sixteen stocks have exceeded the S&P for their respective time frames—and seven have *declined in price* by an average of 53 percent during the greatest bull market in modern history.

Why do highly popular stocks usually end up as costly disappointments? There are two reasons.

First, exciting new markets often don't keep growing as rapidly and profitably as investors expect. This happened to NBI, which was a pioneer in word processing along with Wang Laboratories. After just a few years of success for word processing machines, the personal computer burst on the scene and made stand-alone word processors totally obsolete, because PCs offered full word processing capability as well as broad data processing ability.

Similarly, although the collection and disposal of toxic wastes, as done by Rollins Environmental (now Laidlaw Environmental), experienced rapidly growing demand when governments imposed strict environmental restrictions, the high cost of those services caused businesses to reduce the amount of hazardous materials they generated. So before long, growth for the disposal contractors slowed markedly and competition intensified.

The second reason popular company stocks often disappoint is that when a business achieves great success, competitors, some-

| | | Original P/E Ratio On | | Change from Original Year to 6/98 (%) | |
| | | Stock | S&P 500 | Stock | S&P 500 |
April	Highest P/E				
1982	NBI, Inc.	24	7	–98	+875
1983	Cullinane*	44	12	+657	+614
1984	Advanced Micro Devices	35	12	–32	+587
1985	Cullinet*	37	11	+783	+503
1986	Marion Labs†	53	16	+216	+356
1987	Marion Labs†	68	21	+45	+274
1988	Rollins Environmental‡	34	15	–78	+321
1989	Century Telephone	34	12	+165	+270
1990	Total Systems Services	47	13	+294	+221
1991	U.S. Surgical	63	15	–31	+191

		ORIGINAL P/E RATIO ON		CHANGE FROM ORIGINAL YEAR TO 6/98 (%)	
APRIL	HIGHEST P/E	STOCK	S&P 500	STOCK	S&P 500
1992	U.S. Surgical	70	18	-65	+170
1993	Home Depot	58	18	+147	+147
1994	AnnTaylor Stores	51	20	-42	+124
1995	Corrections Corp.	57	15	+300	+118
1996	Checkpoint Systems	61	17	-28	+68
1997	Cardinal Health	41	19	+25	+45
	AVERAGE	49	15	+141	+305

* Cullinane Database Systems changed its name to Cullinet Software in 1983 and merged into Computer Associates in 1989.
† Marion Labs changed its name to Marion Merrell Dow (MMD) in 1989 when Dow Chemical acquired 76% of Marion's stock. MMD was totally acquired in 1995 by Hoechst. Assume price since 1995 has matched S&P 500.
‡ Name changed in May 1997 to Laidlaw Environmental.

times very powerful ones, are attracted to the field. This slows growth and shrinks profit margins for the early leaders. This happened to Advanced Micro Devices as Intel and some smaller firms developed superior micro-processor chips, and to U.S. Surgical when Johnson & Johnson saw the advantages of la-parascopic surgical instruments and poured huge resources into developing good products for that market. Intel and J&J are now num-ber one in their respective fields, to the detri-ment of AMD and U.S. Surgical (which sold out to Tyco in late 1998—an admission that the bloom was off its rose).

Several of the former market favorites on my list have evolved into strong blue-chip investments and are well regarded today. But overall, their record is dismal. Investors would have been far better off avoiding all of them and following a proven, sensible strat-egy that considered valuation as well as business fundamentals. So when someone tells you, "You've got to own this stock, it's going to be a big winner," watch out. Gotta-own stocks are likely losers, and the reason is simple: investors' enthusiasm for them has pushed their valuations up to illogical, ridiculous extremes.

To avoid the perils of popularity, you should try to recognize when an individual stock, a whole group of stocks, or the entire market has been caught up in a frenzy of excessive optimism. This is not difficult. First, of course, check the valuation of the stock or stocks. If it is way out of line with historical levels, as discussed in the previous chapter, the answer is obvious. Second, track "the buzz." If lots of people are talking up a stock, a group of stocks, or the overall market, watch out. A simple rule is: don't ever buy a stock you hear someone raving about at the water cooler, at a cocktail party, or on the Internet.

Years ago, before so much data went on line, we had a great measure of stock popularity in our office: the thick file/thin file status of various companies. Those whose research folders were bulging with brokers' research reports all recommending Buy and company press releases saying how well the company was doing were excessively popular. Those with thin files and little or no positive information, of course, were out of favor.

Which to buy and which to sell were obvious. The thickest file I ever saw was that of National Student Marketing (NSM) in the late 1960s, during the "Go-Go Market." NSM recruited college students to sell coffee mugs, beer glasses, banners, T-shirts, and other paraphernalia to fellow students. The company had a great public relations operation and it put together a few years of good earnings growth that made the stock extremely popular—but the business lacked staying power and soon collapsed, wiping out all its shareholders.

The Perils of IPOs

One area of popularity to be avoided like the plague is initial public offerings (IPOs). When young, privately financed companies decide to sell stock to the public, they always pick a time when their operating results are particularly favorable and investor interest in their type of business is great. Moreover, most IPOs come when the whole stock market has been pushed up by a surge of investor optimism. That means stock valuations generally are high. This is shown by the record since 1982 when the great secular bull market of the 1980s and 1990s began.

THE EBBS AND FLOWS OF IPOS

	S&P 500 PRICE	YEAR'S IPOS ($BILLION)
1982 Low	102	30.1
1986 High	255	61.8
1990 Low	295	23.4
1993 High	471	111.1
1994 Low	439	60.2
*1998 High	1187	156.4

* First six months, IPOs at annual rate.

Because of their popularity and the risks inherent in young, unseasoned companies, *on average* IPOs perform very badly after the initial burst of enthusiasm. In 1994, Prof. Jay R. Ritter and Tim Loughran published a comprehensive study of the 4753 IPOs traded on the New York Stock Exchange, American Stock Exchange, and NASDAQ between 1970 and 1990. It showed an average annual return for these IPOs of 3.0 percent, three quarters less than the 11.3 percent return of the S&P 500!

All the other studies I've seen show similar results. Technology addicts, who flock to IPOs like bees to honey, should ponder this example from a 1998 *Fortune* article* on Kleiner Perkins Caufield & Byers (KP), generally considered to be one of the shrewdest, most successful venture capital firms in Silicon Valley:

> Between 1990 and 1997, KP took public 79 infotech and life sciences companies that have not been acquired since. If you'd bought each of those stocks immediately after the first day of trading, you would have lost money on 55 of them. That's right, a loser rate of 70%.
>
> If you'd invested $100 in each of the 79 companies, you'd now have $11,716; if you'd invested that $7900 in a fund tracking the NASDAQ Index, you'd have $15,718 . . .

* Reprinted from the October 26, 1998 issue of *Fortune* by special permission; copyright 1998, Time Inc.

The dirty little secret is that VCs (venture capitalists) can be enormously successful even though most of their portfolio companies may tank in the public markets. This stems from the fact that VCs make money on almost any company that gets to an IPO, because as early private-stage investors, they've likely bought the stock at a price three or four times lower than the public offering price.

So buying IPOs, even from the Tiffany of Silicon Valley, is a loser's game. The high valuations on IPOs that usually cause them to do poorly in the market should be obvious to any careful observer. But very few investors—professionals included—understand the poor operating results produced by a majority of IPO companies after their shares have been sold to investors.

My former partner, Peter Schliemann, has done two landmark studies on this subject, in 1989 and 1995. The second study covered 452 of the 513 IPOs that came to market three years earlier, in 1992. Adequate data was unavailable on the rest, which tells us something about the quality of IPOs. The results of this analysis were:

1. Very few companies in the class of 1992 improved on their fundamental sales and earnings trends after going public. Only

14 percent showed such improvement, while 69 percent had deteriorating trends. The rest were constant.

2. Most of the IPO companies achieved peak profit margins within four quarters before or after their offerings. Almost 80 percent fell into that category, but 60 percent then experienced a marked slippage in profitability within two years of the IPO.

3. Over half (58 percent) of the companies had a quarterly earnings *drop* in the first four quarters after their IPOs. Over 75 percent had a decline within two years.

4. Most of the earnings slumps were caused by profit margin problems, but one third of the companies had a sales decline within four quarters, and 45 percent within two years.

5. As with the 1989 group, one of the most troublesome findings was that 19 percent of the companies actually *lost money* in one of the first four quarters after their IPOs. This comparison excluded all companies that lost money throughout the period, or that had normal seasonal losses, so it was even more frightening.

6. One company in four lost money throughout the period under review, both in the years leading up to the IPO as well as in

the years following. This raises the question of whether these companies were ready for the public market if two years later they were still in the red. Even worse were the twenty-three companies that had a few profitable quarters coincident with the IPO, but that then reverted to their money-losing ways.

As one might expect, with such a poor fundamental record following their initial sales to the public (remember that this was a period of good economic growth), the average stock performance of these IPOs was dismal. In the two-year period, half the 513 companies' stocks fell below their offering prices. A higher percentage (56 percent) declined from their prices at the close of the first day's trading. However, since the market in general has done reasonably well since 1992, an even higher number of these IPOs lagged the overall market. Using the S&P 500 as a market proxy, 57 percent of the IPO stocks underperformed from the initial offering, and 64 percent underperformed from the close on the first day of trading.

The lure of IPOs is the understandable desire to find "the next Microsoft" and get in on the ground floor so that an initial investment of $10,000 will grow to $1 million within ten years or less. But people trying to do that might as well be buying lottery tickets, because for every Microsoft there are hundreds of Ashton-Tates and Borlands— Roman candles that soar brightly into the sky and then sink swiftly into the sea. So an excellent rule for investors is: NEVER BUY AN IPO (except for those extremely rare offerings of big, successful companies like Lucent or Conoco that are being spun off by a larger firm for some unusual reason).

Mutual Fund Popularity

Mutual funds are just as subject to overpopularity as individual stocks. Their risks usually aren't as great because of their diversified portfolios. Nevertheless, it's wise not to buy into any fund after it has become popular, as measured by the volume of incoming cash. A January 1998 study by Morningstar showed that "In 21 out of 27 time periods (from 1987 to 1996) unpopular funds went on to beat the average equity fund during the following one, two, and three years. They outran popular funds in 24 out of 27 cases." This happened because typically a fund does not become popular and caught up in the buzz until it's had a stellar record for some time, often several years or longer. Then new money pours into the fund just as its performance peaks and starts to regress to its less exciting norm.

Perception vs. Reality

All that we've said about the excessive enthusiasm for particular stocks or stock groups that leads to their overvaluation is meant to show how *perception* gets totally detached from *reality*. In their infatuation with some exciting new business or concept (like "the environment"), investors stray from the sensible, logical reasoning that I have emphasized is so important. Case in point: when the mania for gambling companies pushed their stocks into the stratosphere in the mid-1990s, their eager buyers neglected to figure out that to make the stocks pay off every river in America would have to be dotted with gambling boats and many millions of new gamblers would have to be enticed aboard them.

The conclusion from this and the many other passionate love affairs investors have had with popular stocks over the years is simple: *be realistic.*

Chapter 9

THE BEST VIEW IS FROM THE BOTTOM

Many investors believe that to be successful they must be like sages sitting on the mountaintop, able to forecast accurately the broad trends that will take place in the financial markets, the overall economy, and specific sectors of the economy. Their goal is to seek out likely areas of greatest economic strength and to concentrate their stock holdings in them.

In theory, this "top-down" approach is fine, but in practice it's difficult to predict future trends until they're well under way. The fact is that forecasts in almost any field are usually extrapolations of trends already in place. This can be seen from the writings of such futurists as Herman Kahn, of the Hudson Institute, some years ago, and John Naisbit more recently. Some of these futurists gain a wide following and their books become best-sellers. But the notable thing about most is that the trends they predict are almost always well established and at least starting to be recognized by investors. Aside from the unusually perceptive Peter Drucker, who started talking about "The Knowledge Society" some two decades ago, almost no one recognized how important computer technology would become until the early 1990s when the power of the personal computer and the Internet became overwhelmingly evident. So most investors got onto that bandwagon *after* information technology stocks had risen sharply, which they did in a sudden surge.

Nor were the other two sweeping trends of the 1990s—the growing internationalization of business and the increasing strength of the United States as a world competitor— recognized by many investors soon enough to take full advantage of them. In the late 1980s and early 1990s, most observers were still worried about foreign competition, viewing it as a negative rather than the strong positive it became as the U.S. developed into the most efficient, most competitive economy in a world where more and more business moved across national borders. And by the time that sea change became obvious, the beneficiaries of it already had fairly high share prices.

A good example of how forecasts of future trends are often mere extrapolations of the recent past is the August 24–31 1998 issue of *Business Week*. The lead article, "The 21st Century Economy," identified the following primary trends for the new century:

- A surge of innovation, including "a much broader flowering of technological, business, and financial creativity"
- A major impact from biotechnology
- "A wholesale rejuvenation of business, financial service firms and universities"
- Increasing globalization
- "Major dislocations and uncertainty for workers and businesses . . . as new technologies are adopted"
- New management thrusts, including focus on the customer, pursuing acquisitions, creating alliances with partners, and using broad-based stock option plans to reward and retain key employees

Every one of these "trends" had already been in place for a long time (up to a decade in many instances) before this article was written.

Projecting the recent past into the future is something investors do all the time, and it often gets them into trouble.

However, the difficulty with top-down investing lies less with the failure to anticipate trends before they reach full flower than it does with the market popularity and high stock valuations that well-recognized trends quickly produce. As always, this reduces the risk/reward ratio of the stocks involved, making them less likely to be really profitable investments, and often potentially *dangerous* investments.

Witness "emerging markets" stocks in the early 1990s. The spread of capitalism and free markets through Latin America and Eastern Asia had been going on for some time before the Berlin Wall came down in 1989 and communism fell in Eastern Europe and the Soviet Union. Thus, this process was well under way by the time most investors latched onto it in 1993 as a new trend. Emerging markets' stocks then skyrocketed to very high valuation levels that made them vulnerable to any hint of a problem. Such a problem soon arose in December 1994, when the overheating of Mexico's financial market caused a collapse in the value of the peso and an economic retrenchment that took three years to overcome.

The inevitable result was a precipitous decline in all emerging markets stocks. That had just about run its course by mid-1997, when the widely admired strength of the East Asian economies was suddenly undermined by the fallout from excessive investment from the West. So for a second time, emerging markets stocks went into free fall.

The same thing had happened 15 years earlier when the universally acknowledged worldwide oil shortage suddenly turned into a surplus. The belief in a shortage had been fostered by continual political turmoil in the Middle East during the 1960s and 1970s, including two wars and one embargo on oil shipments by the Arab countries, plus persistent efforts by the Organization of Petroleum Exporting Countries (OPEC) to restrict production in order to raise prices further. Prices had doubled between 1979 and 1981, after having tripled in the previous six years, and the consensus of the experts in 1981 was that by the mid-1980s crude oil would double again, to $75 a barrel.

In this environment, investors loaded up on oil stocks, driving their prices up so much that the energy category accounted for 30 percent of the total market value of the S&P 500 by 1980, over triple where it had been a decade earlier and four times its 7½ percent weighting in 1998. This was by far the greatest extreme to which any industry sector has ever been carried. (Even with the

huge popularity of the technology group in
recent years, it only accounts for 19 percent
of the S&P's aggregate value in early 1999.)
The frenzy for this sweeping trend was so
great that investors paid as much attention
to the semiannual meetings of the OPEC oil
ministers as they now devote to the monthly
meetings of the Federal Reserve's Open Market Committee—but, in the end, to no avail.
As the normal forces of supply and demand
overcame political influences, the perceived
shortage of oil disappeared overnight and oil
stocks fell before investors could realize that
another "trend" had bitten the dust. By 1996,
oil prices were down 60 percent and the industry's problem was surplus, not shortage.

Even predictions about the general economy are a shaky basis for making investment decisions. Despite their complex
computer models and other sophisticated
new analytical tools, economists still are not
very good at predicting ups and downs in
business activity. Almost always recessions
start before their advent is recognized—and
often advances in business activity proceed
more rapidly and continue longer than forecast. This is why investors in cyclical stocks
are usually at least half a step behind events.

The same is true for countries outside the
U.S. No one we know predicted the long economic slump that began in Japan during the

early 1990s. Nor did many foresee the economic revival of continental Europe in 1998. In fact, through much of 1997, the general attitude about Europe's stagnation was one of despair. As a result of these forecasting failures, few people got out of Japanese stocks before they suddenly fell 46 percent in 1990, or into European stocks before they began to soar in the second half of 1997.

Why "Trends" Are Tricky

There are several reasons major economic and business trends are so hard to forecast. Most important is that the free markets that now dominate the world's economy contain powerful self-correcting forces. Stimulated by the profit motive, capital can flow freely and quickly to areas of opportunity—and just as fast away from areas that begin to look unfavorable. So, for example, if there appears to be a shortage of oil, more exploration activity is financed and more is invested in improving drilling technology to increase the odds of exploration success.

This happened in a major way during the 1970s, as rising oil prices led to the development of huge new oil and gas fields in the North Sea and the North Slope of Alaska. Aiding those discoveries was the application of new computer technology to drilling by oil service companies like Schlumberger and Halliburton. So the oil shortage soon proved to be an illusion.

In similar fashion, the U.S. industrial companies located in what became known as the Rust Belt during the 1980s unexpectedly, but more or less inevitably, responded to foreign competitive pressures by restructuring on a large scale, investing in new equipment, improving their efficiency, and pursuing foreign markets more aggressively. This was how America's auto, machinery, and steel producers got back into the game as viable players. This was not enough of a transformation to make many of those businesses great investments, because they still operate in difficult industries, as pointed out in Chapter 3. However, the remarkable revival of the Rust Belt has provided a major lift to the American economy, allowing it to do better in the 1990s than most people had forecast.

Another reason broad trends of any type are hard to predict is that people's thinking is strongly influenced by what is happening *now* and what has happened in the recent past. That makes it difficult for any but the boldest analyst to forecast major changes and demonstrate why they're going to happen.

Consider beliefs about inflation, for example. By the early 1980s, we had experienced high inflation at rates from 6 to 13.5 percent for so long that it seemed impossible to believe that annual rises in the Consumer Price Index could ever get back to 3 to 4 percent, let alone under 2 percent, as they did in the late 1990s. So top-down investors clung grimly for too long to inflation hedge investments such as natural resources and gold, once more missing a crucial switch in the trend.

This is not to say investors should ignore major economic and business trends. Obviously, these deserve close attention, because it is important to understand what is going on today, even if that's not a useful tool for predicting the future. Moreover, it's very important to realize how strongly a particular trend has captured investors' fancy, so as to avoid the excessive enthusiasm and high stock valuations the trend du jour has fostered.

A Better Way

Given all the difficulties with top-down investing, is there a better way? Yes, there is: the *bottom-up approach,* which I recommend for most investors. Put simply, this strategy involves focusing on the analysis of different companies *as business enterprises* and assessing their valuation in the stock market.

Most of the really successful investors, like Warren Buffett and Peter Lynch, have used this approach. They have sought out companies with favorable business characteristics that were reasonably valued, or truly cheap, and put their money into them.

True, not all their selections turned out to be winners, but their batting averages were high, because they concentrated primarily on factual information that could be analyzed with a high degree of accuracy. So when Buffett studied Coca-Cola, Gillette, and the very successful property/casualty insurance companies GEICO and General Re, he could see the competitive strengths in those companies' products and services and the excellent growth they had achieved. Then he had to determine the odds of their future success if the companies' managements continued to perform well. This task did require judgment, but not sheer guesswork about the future.

Finally, Buffett had to determine what was a realistic valuation to pay for these stocks. That, too, involved a degree of judgment, but it was based on all the historical data on past market valuation patterns, of the type that will be described in the next chapter. This was factual information, and the main element of judgment was whether past patterns of valuation would recur in the future—or, if not, how they might vary and why.

Similarly, when Peter Lynch made his famous investment in Sara Lee, because of the potential growth in l'Eggs pantyhose, he analyzed the market for that type of product, studied the advantages of the unique way l'Eggs were being presented in plastic "shells" to store customers, reviewed the characteristics of Sara Lee's other product lines, forecast the growth prospects for the company as a whole, and then did his valuation analysis. All of this led to a buy decision that was based largely on known facts.

One might think a bottom-up investor would accumulate a portfolio of miscellaneous stocks scattered all over the map. But this is rarely the case. The reason is that while industry groups of stocks tend to move in different directions at different times, all the stocks within a group tend to move together. Accordingly, when a particular group of good-quality companies becomes reasonably valued in the market, the bottom-up investor will buy at least several stocks in that sector.

This happened to bank and insurance companies in 1990 when severe loan losses (especially in real estate) depressed the prices of *all* bank and insurance shares, regardless of their strength and skill in avoiding such large loan losses. This created great buying opportunities in top-drawer stocks like BancOne, NationsBank, American International Group, and General Re, which astute bottom-up investors bought eagerly because of the favorable combination of attractive business fundamentals and low valuation.

A similar surge of buying interest by bottom-up investors developed in drug stocks during 1993–1994, after that group of stocks had been hammered by investor worries about pricing restraints on pharmaceuticals stemming from growing emphasis on "managed care" and Hillary Clinton's proposed health care reform program. As these concerns proved to be overblown, drug stocks took off and the inherent strengths of the industry reasserted themselves.

By the end of 1996, when most sectors of the market had risen sharply and investor optimism was high, one of the few industry groups that had lagged was retail stocks. This was because consumers were not spending, since wage increases were slow and people were worried about losing their jobs in restructuring programs. The reasonable valuations of even top store chains like Wal-Mart, Home Depot, and Walgreen registered on the bottom-up investors' screens and they were quick to purchase those stocks at what turned out to be very favorable prices.

So, over just a few years, the bottom-up approach led these investors to make broad commitments in three good industry sectors. And during the 1990s, there have also been periods when temporary drops in technology issues and consumer products stocks like Cisco, Colgate, Gillette, Lucent, PepsiCo, and McDonald's have attracted the disciplined buyer looking for both strong business fundamentals and reasonable valuation.

As a result, bottom-up investors were able to accumulate well diversified stock portfolios without relying on the uncertain, risky practice of forecasting broad future trends.

Chapter 10

SPREADING
YOUR BETS

Like motherhood, diversification of stock investments is generally considered to be "a good thing." And it is, but not just because it is a protective device. Clearly, it is desirable to own a variety of companies in at least half a dozen different industries. This reduces the risk of a big hit to the portfolio's overall value if a particular company or industry hits an air pocket. So, spreading your bets, or not putting all your eggs in one basket, makes a lot of sense. But there's also another, generally overlooked, positive reason to diversify: Spreading your bets over enough potential winners can increase your odds of hitting at least a few big ones.

Among the many thousands of publicly traded stocks, there have to be more than five or ten that will be extremely rewarding in the future, so investors who limit their selections to just a handful of companies are greatly reducing their odds of success. This has proven out time after time with both industry and company diversification.

For example, bank stocks have rarely been considered promising growth investments, because that is a slow-growing, competitive business—and one subject to unexpected serious loan losses every ten years or so. However, the consolidation of the banking industry helped the stocks perform extremely well in 1996 and 1997. In fact, bank shares rose more in price than just about any other major group, advancing about 50 percent in both 1996 and 1997.

Thus, investors who had no stake in that important market sector missed out on its substantial appreciation and their portfolios had a hard time keeping up with the market in those years. Bank stocks did hit an air pocket in the second half of 1998 as a few big institutions took large unexpected loan losses, but the strongest banks will rebound and be good investments in the future.

Technology stocks also illustrate the point. Following an initial surge of growth, the personal computer industry went into a slump in the late 1980s, while both the mainframe and minicomputer markets stagnated. All technology stocks slumped badly and the industry became unpopular with investors, many of whom sold all their stocks in that sector. Then, as major advances in microprocessor technology, networking, and software gave the PC business new impetus in the early and mid-1990s, those investors found themselves out of a rejuvenated market sector that was running away from them. Lacking diversification in technology, many people missed the strongest phase of that group's upsurge.

However, having adequate industry diversification does not require owning something in a dozen or more industry groups. In fact, going much beyond ten sectors inevitably puts one into the average or below-average industries listed in Chapter 3. Owning airline, auto, or steel stocks can be profitable occasionally, but not frequently enough to justify including them in a diversified portfolio seeking above-average long-term growth.

Some diversification *within* attractive industry groups is also desirable to spread one's bets. This is particularly important in the pharmaceutical field, which contains a number of well-managed companies, all doing excellent research. No one could have predicted fifteen years ago that Eli Lilly would develop a blockbuster antidepressant (Prozac) or five years ago that Pfizer would come up with such a winner as Viagra in a brand-new therapeutic category. But they did, and well-diversified drug stock portfolios owned one or both of those stocks.

Similarly, a well-thought-out list of technology stocks in 1996 would have included Intel, Cisco, Microsoft, Compaq, Motorola, and Hewlett-Packard. Of those stocks, the first three did really well in the next three years, but the others were disappointing.

Within other industries, where only a few outstanding companies are well entrenched, diversification is not necessary. In soft drinks, Coca-Cola and PepsiCo are most of the game. The same is true in household products with Colgate, Procter & Gamble, and Clorox; personal care with Gillette; home and building supplies with Home Depot (and Lowe's a notch below); and Walgreen and CVS in drugstores.

So an important part of the investor's analytical task is to determine how many participants in a fundamentally attractive industry have, and are likely to maintain, leadership positions that will enable their stocks to do well.

For investors with limited assets, certainly under $50,000, the only way to obtain adequate diversification is to invest in mutual funds, but no more than two to four. For the investor who buys individual stocks for a medium-sized portfolio, the early goal should be to own at least ten stocks in no less than five different industries. That will provide minimally adequate protection against unhappy surprises and a fair spread of bets on future winners. For large portfolios, good diversification can be achieved with thirty to forty stocks (i.e., 2½ to 3 percent positions on average). Unless one is going to own small companies, any number much above forty will dilute the favorable impact of one's best selections.

Once a portfolio has been assembled and time passes, the initial diversification will become skewed as the best-performing stocks and industry groups increase their weightings. Up to a point, this is fine because more often than not, today's winners will continue to do well in the future—not every year, but on average over time. So it's usually a mistake to cut back on the largest holdings just to stick to a fixed diversification lineup.

On this subject, Gerald Loeb, one of the wisest investment commentators of the 1950s and 1960s, recommended a strategy that has really stood the test of time: *cut your losses and let your profits run.* He urged selling disappointing stocks after they had been given a fair chance to get back on track, but staying with one's best performers even as they became proportionately much larger holdings in a long-term portfolio. In his excellent book, *The Battle for Investment Survival,* Loeb wrote, "Accepting losses is the most important single investment device to insure safety of capital."

This approach, of course, also has tax advantages. Realizing losses on losers saves taxes and holding onto winners avoids paying lots of taxes on realized gains. Longstanding, mature portfolios show the advantage of letting diversification evolve this way, while always looking, of course, for new areas of attraction to put money into.

In 1998, we reviewed the portfolio of a client whose assets we had managed for thirty years. It was sort of an anniversary party, and a happy one for this sixty-five-year-old who was about to retire. The equity account had outperformed the S&P 500 by a moderate amount, a good showing for any portfolio, and most of the superior results had been produced by four stocks that had been purchased in the early days of our management: Abbott Laboratories, Merck, General Electric, and Gillette. Each of these stocks had lagged behind the market at times along the way (in the case of Gillette, for seven long years from 1973 to 1980), but the companies had maintained their basic strengths and in recent years the stocks had all come on strong.

The striking point from a diversification perspective is that "letting our profits run" meant that in 1998 these four stocks accounted for just over 50 percent of the total market value of the portfolio (between 10 percent and 14 percent each). Had Abbott, Merck, GE, and Gillette not been such powerful companies, we would have cut the size of their holdings in this portfolio somewhat over the years, but each operates in good businesses where we wanted sizable stakes, so the risk of such large holdings looked like a reasonable one—especially recognizing the large tax penalty of doing any selling. (All have tax costs of $1.50 per share or less.)

To counterbalance the very large weighting in those stocks, we adjusted the rest of the diversification from time to time, so the portfolio in 1998 was well spread out in most respects, the only area of potential concern being a very high weighting in health care, which we watched carefully.

Well as this portfolio has done, it's had some turkeys along the way, which eventually were dumped to take advantage of their tax losses. But diversification greatly reduced the negative impact of our boo-boos.

Another point on taking losses is worth mentioning. Some investors hate to sell any stock at a loss. To them, it's admitting defeat;

so they try to hold on until the stock recovers to their cost price. Then they sell. This is the "thank goodness I'm even" syndrome, and it makes no sense. If the company concerned is no longer an attractive long-term investment, it's much better to move out and get into one that is achieving good sales and earnings growth. The latter's stock, if reasonably valued, is likely to be advancing while the investor waits for the laggard to get back to its initial cost. Often that's a long wait.

International Diversification

Another important form of equity diversification is having a stake in foreign companies that are headquartered outside the United States. There are three reasons to do this.

First, not all the world's best companies are American, and restricting one's investments to U.S. firms screens out many strong, well-run companies. Big and important as American businesses are on the global scene, the aggregate market value of all non-U.S. companies' shares accounts for half the total value of the combined world stock markets. So it doesn't make sense to overlook such a huge area of opportunity—even though many large U.S.-based companies do get sizable portions of their sales and earnings from foreign countries.

Second, economic growth is basically faster in many other nations, despite the temporary setbacks that occur there (as in Asia during the late 1990s). It makes sense to take advantage of that growth through foreign-based companies.

Third, various stock markets around the world don't always move in sync, so international diversification smoothes out a stock portfolio's returns. For example, in 1997 the European, Brazilian, and Mexican markets outpaced the strong performance of U.S. equities, while Asian stocks lagged.

Shifts in currency values do increase or reduce the returns of foreign stocks when translated into U.S. dollars, but over time much of the impact of those swings washes out.

More and more of the large foreign-based companies now have their shares traded on the New York Stock Exchange as well as on their home markets, which is a great convenience for U.S. investors.

To spread both risks and opportunities, it's important to diversify *within* the international component of a portfolio. To accomplish this, most individual investors should use one or two mutual funds to obtain their international exposure.

PART IV

AVOIDING PITFALLS

Chapter 11

WHAT PEOPLE
WORRY ABOUT
TOO MUCH

Risk is an inevitable part of equity investing and it's a difficult subject for many
people to understand. As a result, some investors overemphasize its significance, and
others—especially in ebullient markets like
that of 1996–1999—underestimate it.

The fact is that while there are many
kinds of risks in stocks, most of them can be
handled in a way that reduces the overall
risk of an equity portfolio to a modest level.
Thus, it is possible to achieve favorable investment performance over a period of years
without exposing one's valuable capital to
high risk.

Moreover, the longer an investor's perspective—whether dealing with an institutional portfolio or a personal one—the less
he or she has to worry about risk. To under-

stand this, let's analyze the various kinds of equity risks.

Company Risks

The fundamental basis of business is competition. So, to be successful, companies must continually sustain the quality and effectiveness of their products or services at a high level, and keep down the cost of those products or services. Otherwise, they won't hold their own in the market against other suppliers.

Occasionally firms just experience bad luck—someone else develops a breakthrough product or a market matures unexpectedly— but usually when a company's competitive position slips, it is because of poor management. Such lapses, which cause earnings to slump and lead to bad stock performance, can occur at any time but are more likely to come when there's a major change going on in a particular business. At those points managements of previously successful companies may become complacent, fail to recognize the implications of a new development, and continue to follow the comfortable path of the past.

Obviously Sears, Roebuck greatly underestimated the impact of discount retailing when it burst on the scene in the late 1960s.

Management did almost nothing to adjust to this new form of competition, so Sears and its stock were poor performers for the next twenty years. Similarly, when PCs and workstations were developed during the 1970s and 1980s, the managements of Digital Equipment and IBM greatly misunderstood the impact of the microcomputer on their minicomputer and mainframe product lines.

On the other hand, Hewlett-Packard (for years the second largest minicomputer producer) recognized the great potential of the microcomputer. Rather than sit back and be hurt by this new product, the company adapted its product lines to capitalize on some of the vast applications the microcomputer would develop. And in addition to developing good PCs and workstations, HP charged into the printer field and soon became the dominant firm in that business.

Although consumer markets are more stable and serious competition from new consumer products is less frequent, it does occur. Many years ago Procter & Gamble successfully entered a new market (for P&G) by introducing Crest, a superior toothpaste endorsed by the American Dental Association. This dealt a temporary setback to Colgate, which had long been the leader.

Gillette and Intel are two examples of companies whose managements have been very adept at obsoleting their own products before competitors do. This is why they have the best growth and highest profit margins in their fields. Even Gillette's biggest fans were surprised when the company introduced the Sensor Excel—a distinctly superior version of the Sensor razor—just 3½ years after the extremely successful 1990 launch of the original Sensor. And then, five years later, the company came out with the radically different Mach3. This is an excellent example of preempting potential competition. Similarly, Intel has continued to dominate the fast-moving microchip market by developing and introducing advanced new chips every three years or so.

Cost control is also important in the competitive battle. It has always impressed me how highly efficient firms like General Electric and Emerson Electric press ever harder each year to reduce their costs further—and do so with great success.

In other companies, though, it has taken a true crisis and plummeting stock prices to spur effective action on efficiency improvement. Ford and Chrysler had to be teetering on the edge of bankruptcy in the early 1980s before they confronted their cumbersome operating methods and high costs vis-à-vis the Japanese. And it wasn't until General Motors got into a real financial bind in 1992 that the directors bit the bullet and forced a drastic management shake-up in that slumping company, aimed at attacking a bloated cost structure and poor vehicle design.

Between the extremes of good and bad, a number of substantial, seasoned companies slip a bit competitively from time to time for product or cost reasons. However, as we pointed out in Chapter 5, they usually pull themselves together before too long and get back onto their previous track of success.

Looking at the record, you will find that among well-established large and medium-sized firms, the number that get into long-term difficulty (like Sears, Eastman Kodak, and General Motors) is really quite small. Moreover, as some recent positive developments at those companies show, even persistent underachievers have a good chance of rebounding eventually. This is especially true now that large institutional investors are actively pressing companies to perform well. So, in most instances, the patient investor will find that company risk is relatively low among sizable companies that have been successful for a long time. And this kind of risk can easily be minimized by diversification and careful company analysis.

Among small companies, though, business risk is much higher—especially for firms that have not been around for many years and don't have well-tested managements. Even long-lived small companies tend to have narrow product lines, so a real problem in any one of them is likely to cause the corporate equivalent of pneumonia, whereas it would produce only the sniffles for a General Electric (as with its ill-fated purchase of Kidder Peabody) or a heavy cold for a company such as Air Products. Because of the higher risk level of small firms, anyone investing in their stocks definitely should have a broadly diversified group of holdings.

Currency Risk

Since the transformation in 1971 of the post-World War II Bretton Woods international monetary system, which was aimed at limiting fluctuations in the values of different countries' currencies, the foreign exchange market has been subject to wide gyrations. This can have a substantial impact on the reported earnings and balance sheet values of companies that do business in different nations.

When the dollar is strong versus other countries' currencies, a U.S. company's foreign earnings are worth less after being translated into dollars; but when our currency is weak, overseas profits are worth more dollars. This is particularly significant, of course, to the big U.S. multinational firms, which today earn one third, one half, or even more of their profits abroad.

The following table shows how currency shifts have affected the reported earnings of one large American-based multinational firm, Minnesota Mining and Manufacturing (3M). Positive or negative currency impacts of 2 to 7 percent may not seem like much, but for a company whose earnings generally grow at about 8 to 10 percent per year, the effect on one year's profit (and, for a while, on the stock price) can be significant.

Many companies hedge against at least part of their currency risk in the derivatives

3M COMPANY: FOREIGN CURRENCY IMPACT PER SHARE

	OPERATING EARNINGS ($)	FOREIGN CURRENCY ($)	REPORTED EARNINGS ($)	CURRENCY IMPACT (%)
1998	4.09	−0.35	3.74	−8.6
1997	4.15	−0.27	3.88	−6.5
1996	3.78	−0.15	3.63	−4.0
1995	3.13	+0.10	3.23	+3.2
1994	3.18	None	3.18	None
1993	3.05	−0.14	2.91	−4.6
1992	2.82	None	2.82	None
1991	2.58	+0.05	2.63	+1.9
1990	2.89	+0.07	2.96	+2.4

market in a sensible manner, but when major moves take place in foreign exchange values, even those firms can be affected substantially—and it is not easy to predict such impacts.

The effect of currency swings on foreign stocks can be greater. When an investor in one country puts money into the shares of a company domiciled in another country, that company's shares tend to be traded most actively in its home country. Therefore, shifts in the value of the dollar versus the other nation's currency can seriously influence the dollar price of the foreign stock. For example, if the stock rises 10 percent in its home market but the currency of the country declines 15 percent, the U.S. investor ends up with a loss of 5 percent.

Currency shifts do tend to wash out over time, except where there are extreme differences in inflation and government policies. Also, the risk of adverse currency moves can and should be reduced by diversifying among a number of foreign markets.

Economic Risks

The primary economic danger for stocks comes from the *business cycle*. Severe recessions, such as the one experienced in 1980 to 1982, can temporarily depress the profits of many types of companies, and thus their share prices.

If it were possible to forecast accurately the timing and depth of recessions, it would be easy and profitable to make major moves into cyclical stocks at recession lows and then out near business peaks. However, as we said earlier, business cycles have proven difficult to predict, so investors should be wary of holding cyclical stocks after economic activity has risen to boom levels. And cyclical stocks are also less desirable for individual investors because even if an investor trades in and out of these stocks successfully, capital gains taxes eat up a sizable portion of the profits.

Secular changes in the economy also pose risks for individual stocks, but these are easier to see before they do much damage. For example, many years ago it became apparent that service activities were going to grow much faster than basic manufacturing. Recognition of that fact prompted sensible investors to shift their focus away from what had been pretty good growth sectors in the metals and basic chemicals fields (aluminum, molybdenum, plastics, fertilizer, etc.) toward new areas like computer services and fast-food restaurants.

One did not have to buy Automatic Data Processing or McDonald's when they first went public in 1965 to do well in those stocks. The strong secular economic trends favoring those service businesses have continued, and investors who bought both the stocks even ten years later had achieved more than thirtyfold price appreciation for Automatic Data Processing and twentyfold for McDonald's by 1998. On the other hand, those who held onto even one of the best metals companies, Alcoa, have since 1975 experienced just a fivefold price gain, while the S&P 500 rose fifteenfold.

Other examples of the negative impact of secular changes in the economy on particular industries are (1) the great growth in global competition over the past twenty-five years and (2) the acceleration of technological development in electronic hardware, which now makes superior new products in that field obsolete in two years or less and has greatly increased the company failure rate in computers and related electronic products.

All this points up the importance of paying attention to secular changes in the economy and adjusting investment portfolios to reflect those changes.

Inflation and Interest Rate Risks

The impact of *inflation* on companies and their stocks is such an important part of the economic risk picture that we are discussing it separately. As we saw in the late 1960s and throughout the 1970s, accelerating inflation is a serious problem for both corporate profits and the stock market.

First, when the cost of doing business starts to accelerate, it becomes difficult for many types of companies to maintain their profit margins either by boosting efficiency more rapidly or raising selling prices. This is why corporate operating earnings (excluding the illusory benefit of underdepreciation and inventory gains) showed no net increase all the way from 1965 to 1975.

Poor earnings performance in a period of accelerating inflation is compounded in the stock market by the decline in price/earnings ratios caused by the much higher yields that become available on bonds. This is *interest rate risk*. The dramatically negative impact of higher interest rates on stock valuations and stock prices during the accelerating inflation of 1965 to 1980, and the benefit of decelerating inflation and declining interest rates in the past eighteen years, are shown in the table on page 140.

Note that from 1965 through 1980, stocks appreciated at an average annual rate of only 2.6 percent, just one third of their long-term appreciation rate of 7 percent. Then, when inflation unwound and interest rates fell back, P/Es rose—so the rate of stock appre-

INFLATION AND STOCK PRICES:
ANNUAL AVERAGES

	INFLATION (%)	TEN-YEAR TREASURY YIELD (%)	S&P 500 P/E	S&P 500 PRICE	YEARLY PRICE APPRECIATION (%)
1965	1.6	4.30	16.8	92	
1965–1980					2.6
1980	13.5*	11.46[†]	8.1	136	
1980–1999					12.7
1999 (May)	1.5	4.84	28.0	1330	

* Inflation peak.
[†] All-time high annual average Treasury yield of 13.9% reached in 1981 when inflation was 10.4%.

ciation jumped to 12.7 percent, 80 percent faster than the historical average. This put the average for the thirty-three-year period almost exactly at the long-term norm of 7 percent. Normally, swings in inflation and interest rates are far more moderate than they were from 1965 to 1998. However, at various times they are wide enough to have a significant impact on stock valuations and prices.

Inflation poses a *secular* risk for investors as well as a *cyclical* one. The secular problem is simple: lacking the harsh discipline of the old gold standard, our monetary system and government structure virtually guarantee *some* inflation just about every year. Even if the average rate is fairly low—say 3 percent—over an extended period, it seriously erodes the purchasing power of both the investor's capital and the income stream it produces. A 3 percent rate of inflation boosts the cost of living by 16 percent in five years, 34 percent in ten years, 56 percent in fifteen years, and 81 percent in twenty years. Most individual investors have a time horizon of at least fifteen to twenty years, and institutional investors have a virtually unlimited time frame. So even seemingly low rates of inflation do matter. (We'll talk about this problem more in Chapter 16.)

History proves that common stocks give far more protection to the purchasing power

of capital and the income it generates than
bonds do, because the long-term total return
of stocks is double that of bonds. Therefore,
recognizing the secular trend of inflation,
*the greatest risk for most investors is that
they don't have enough of their capital in
stocks, not that they have too much.*

Political Risk

There are two types of political risk: domestic and international. On the domestic side,
there is the negative impact on business of
the increases in government regulation that
seem to occur regardless of which party is in
power in Washington. Another type of domestic political risk is the large amounts
spent for government-mandated programs—
expenses such as those for well-intentioned
environmental, social, health care, and other
purposes, which businesses have to assume.
Economists' estimates show that the total of
this cost burden is now roughly $600 billion,
equivalent to about two thirds of total pretax
corporate profits—and this figure will probably grow in the future.

Government regulation and mandated
spending do not fall evenly on all types of
companies, so each one has to be evaluated
carefully on this score. Occasionally some
business just plain gets in the sights of gov-

ernment for an unexpected reason, and it can then be hurt by negative political action for a long time. This happened to the natural gas industry when price regulation was imposed way back in the 1950s. In the 1970s and 1980s it happened to the production side of the U.S. oil business as new environmental curbs prevented many offshore development projects as well as exploratory drilling in key areas of Alaska. In the 1990s it happened to the health care industry, as noted in Chapter 6.

International risks are primarily geopolitical. Three times in the past twenty-five years wars in the Middle East have caused sharply higher oil prices, with injurious effects on the U.S. economy as well as other nations' economies. In addition, these crises have had a negative impact on the global financial system.

For decades, the Cold War with the Soviet Union was a continuing economic drain and a source of investment uncertainty. Though the Cold War is over, there are still potentially explosive risky "hot spots" in the world—North Korea, Yugoslavia, the Middle East, Africa, and so on. Nobody can predict where the next major geopolitical disruption will occur, but it's obvious that peace has not spread to every corner of the globe, and if the past is any guide it never will.

Freedom of trade is another area of international political risk. Here, the trends have been favorable for a long time, but the bitter fight in the United States over approval of the North American Free Trade Agreement, the difficult final stages of the latest General Agreement on Tariffs and Trade (GATT) trade negotiations, and continuing trade spats around the world indicate that the forces of protectionism remain strong. If they gain more influence in the future, many nations' economies and stock markets could suffer.

In 1997 to 1998, international risks became a major investment factor. Excessive capital inflows and overinvestment in Asian countries generated a series of financial collapses where weak market and political structures were ill equipped to deal with the crises. Their impact affected other parts of the world, including the U.S.

Investor Psychology Risk

All of the foregoing risks, which are quite specific, affect stock prices. There is also a broader, general market risk: investor attitude, which we refer to time and again in this book. Investor attitude is characterized at its extremes by ebullient optimism and deep pessimism.

As human beings, investors are emotional. And their moods are greatly affected by current economic and financial conditions. When the investment weather is warm and sunny, they feel good; when it's cold and rainy, they feel bad. These mood swings have a great impact on their willingness to buy and own stocks—and thus on the prices of stocks.

At the start of the 1980s, the economy was beset by high inflation and slow economic growth, great disillusionment with the Carter administration, a soaring federal tax burden, a deterioration of American industry's competitiveness, and other discouraging problems. Moreover, stock prices had gone nowhere for a full decade. So investors were in a sour mood and stocks were selling at a near record low price/earnings ratio of 8.

By late summer 1982, though, some of the clouds began to lift. Inflation showed definite signs of decelerating, and for the first time in many years a president (Ronald Reagan) was promising to lower taxes and help business. So investor psychology started to swing toward optimism.

By 1997 and early 1998, we had come full circle. The problems everyone had been worrying about sixteen years ago were long gone. Investors were feeling very confident because of low inflation and interest rates, rising cor-

porate profits, the strong competitive position of American business and, significantly,
the excellent performance of the stock market for a lengthy period. These favorable factors generated an optimistic mood, so stock
valuations rose to a record high level, reaching a price/earnings multiple (on current
earnings) of 28 on the S&P 500 in mid-1998.

But then the festering financial and economic problems in Asia, which had arisen a
year earlier, deteriorated further just as the
Russian economy and political system unexpectedly slid over the cliff. These events had
a negative impact on the earnings of many
U.S. corporations, and the net effect was a
quick shift in investor psychology from un-
bridled optimism to caution and even appre-
hension. Stock prices fell sharply and by
Labor Day the average stock on the New
York Stock Exchange was down over 35 percent from its 1998 high and the average
NASDAQ issue had plummeted 45 percent.

This type of mood shift (which in 1998
didn't last very long) usually occurs at least
once in every decade. The fact is, of course,
that the inherent value of most stocks does
not change very much from one year to the
next. And as earnings and dividends trend
upward, so does the true value of stocks. But
such changes in market psychology create

wide swings in stock prices, above and below their inherent values.

This is illustrated in Figure 11.1 on page 148 and 149. Observe that despite the exceptionally consistent, nearly straight-line growth of ADP's earnings, the stock has experienced major price advances during surges of investor optimism, followed successively by price declines of 27 percent, 41 percent, 23 percent, and 20 percent when the mood became pessimistic. During all these swings absolutely nothing changed to affect the inherent value of ADP's stock—so the price gyrations were due entirely to shifts in investor psychology.

Obviously, if we could predict these mood swings, we would sell stocks before they went down and buy them back when they were poised to rebound. Many investors attempt such "market timing" but, as will be discussed in the next chapter, in the real world that approach fails far more often than it succeeds.

In the short run, stocks are risky investments; their prices can fluctuate widely. But in the long run a well-diversified portfolio of high quality stocks is not risky—especially if it is monitored closely and kept up-to-date by weeding out the occasional faltering companies and cutting back holdings of stocks

AUTOMATIC DATA PROCESSING, INCORPORATED (AUD)

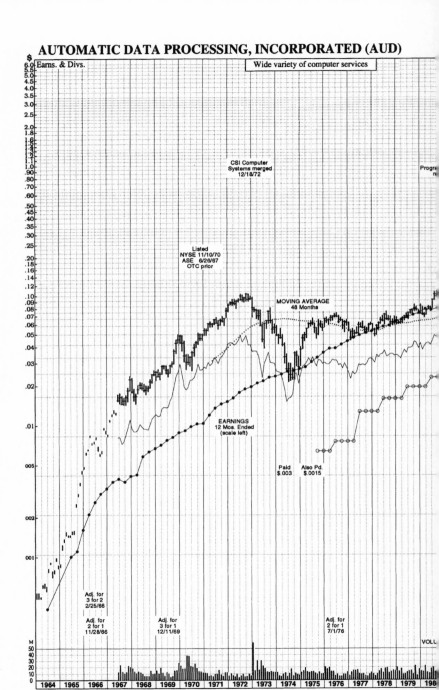

Earns. & Divs.

Wide variety of computer services

CSI Computer
Systems merged
12/18/72

Progr
n

Listed
NYSE 11/10/70
ASE 6/26/67
OTC prior

MOVING AVERAGE
48 Months

EARNINGS
12 Mos. Ended
(scale left)

Paid   Also Pd.
$.003 $.0015

Adj. for
3 for 2
2/25/66

Adj. for
2 for 1
11/28/66

Adj. for
3 for 1
12/11/69

Adj. for
2 for 1
7/1/76

VOLL

M
50
40
30
20
10
0

1964 | 1965 | 1966 | 1967 | 1968 | 1969 | 1970 | 1971 | 1972 | 1973 | 1974 | 1975 | 1976 | 1977 | 1978 | 1979 | 198

Source: Securities Research Company

148

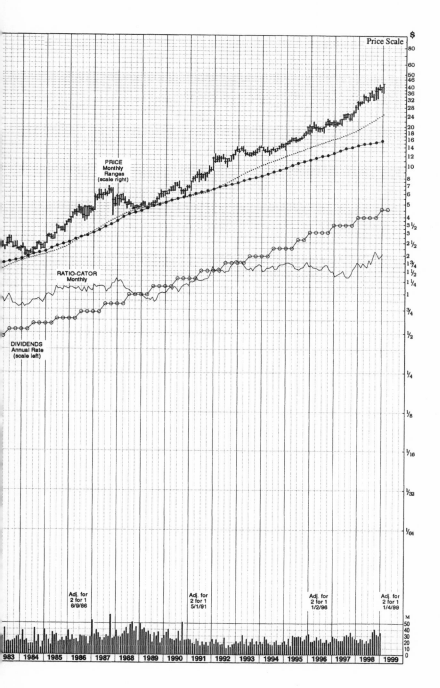

Price Scale $

PRICE
Monthly
Ranges
(scale right)

RATIO-CATOR
Monthly

DIVIDENDS
Annual Rate
(scale left)

80
60
50
46
40
36
32
28

24
20
18
16
14
12
10
8
7
6
5
4
3½
3
2½

2
1¾
1½
1¼

1

¾

½

¼

⅛

1/16

1/32

1/64

Adj. for
2 for 1
8/9/86

Adj. for
2 for 1
5/1/91

Adj. for
2 for 1
1/2/96

Adj. for
2 for 1
1/4/99

M
50
40
30
20
10
0

| 983 | 1984 | 1985 | 1986 | 1987 | 1988 | 1989 | 1990 | 1991 | 1992 | 1993 | 1994 | 1995 | 1996 | 1997 | 1998 | 1999 |

149

that become so popular that they are dangerously overvalued.

It is important to understand that most of the risks that affect stocks—and at times depress their prices rather severely—are transitory. At worst, they wreak damage on a total portfolio for only a small segment of the investor's time frame. People tend to worry too much about the risks in stocks. Of course, they should pay attention to those risks and take sensible measures to minimize them. But their primary focus should be on the positive forces of earnings and dividend growth, which inexorably lead to capital appreciation. Such a focus is particularly beneficial in bear markets, when discouragement and pessimism create the best buying opportunities.

Chapter 12

AN ALMOST CERTAIN WAY TO LOSE MONEY

The phrase "a snare and delusion" was not coined to describe market timing, but no other words better characterize that investment strategy.

Many investors, especially newer ones, believe the only way they can achieve good results with stocks is to be in the market when it's rising and out of the market when it's falling. So they struggle to figure out when to sell many or all of their stocks to avoid the next decline—and when to load up with equities to catch the next upturn.

Unfortunately, many people in the investment business—especially brokers and the publishers of market letters—cater to the quixotic desire of both individual and professional investors to "beat the market" in this fashion. Such a quest is always profitable for the purveyors of timing advice, but rarely so for their clients. In fact, history shows clearly that *market timing is usually counterproductive,* providing poorer results than can be achieved by just buying good stocks at favorable valuation levels and holding them as long as the companies owned continue to do well in their various businesses—merely replacing a few laggards in the portfolio each year to keep it up-to-date.

One study on this subject, published in the Winter 1994 issue of *The Journal of Portfolio Management,* showed that on average a group of twenty-five market timing investment professionals had their clients out of the stock market for *43 percent of the time* between 1985 and 1990, during which period stock prices *doubled.*

In his excellent 1998 book, *Contrarian Investment Strategies: The Next Generation,* David Dreman summarizes the results of 185 market timers (who operate under the new term *tactical asset allocation*) over the 12 years ending in September 1997.

That time span covered a substantial portion of the most recent secular bull market, but it also included the October 1987 crash and the Gulf War slump in 1990. Despite the opportunities those market declines offered timers to get a leg up on steady investors, the timers' aggregate performance was terrible. For the dozen years, their cumulative total return was 384 percent, well below the average return of 589 percent for all domestic equity mutual funds, and *only slightly over half* the 734 percent return of the S&P 500 index. The no-brainer strategy of just investing in the index really won that contest! Other studies of actual portfolio results of market timers show a similar picture.

Here are three principal reasons why any sort of market timing strategy is almost impossible to implement successfully:

1. The long-term trend of the market is strongly upward, paralleling the growth of corporate earnings and dividends as discussed in Chapter 2. Therefore, whenever investors are out of the market they are betting against a powerful trend.

2. Almost all major shifts in market direction after long upward and downward moves are triggered by totally unexpected events. Obviously, these are impossible to predict.

3. Emotion, that old bugaboo of investors, makes it very hard for any human being to bet against the very strong consensus that prevails near market peaks and troughs. Taking the timing plunge is just as difficult as diving into icy waters off the Maine coast.

Let's look first at the inexorable uptrend of the stock market. Data compiled by Ibbotson Associates shows that since 1926 stock prices have risen in:

70 percent of all one-year periods
86 percent of all five-year periods
97 percent of all ten-year periods
100 percent of all fifteen-year periods

Adding to the headwind with which the market's uptrend assails market timers is a striking fact: almost all of the net advance in stock prices over the years has come in short bursts, so being out of the market at *any* time poses a serious risk that the investor will totally miss the boat for a long subsequent period.

In 1994, a University of Michigan study showed that during the three decades from 1963 to 1993, 95 percent of all the market's net gains came in just ninety days, a mere 1.2 percent of all the trading days! Missing those critical days would have reduced an investor's average annual total return from 11.8 percent (had that investor been in the market all the time) to 3.3 percent—less than half of what Treasury bills returned then.

Looking at market timing on a monthly basis, the same study indicated that from

1926 through 1993, missing the best twelve months (1.5 percent of all the months in that sixty-eight-year period) would have lowered one's average annual return from 12.0 percent to 8.1 percent. Being out for the best forty-eight months (5.8 percent of all months) would have shrunk the annual return to a minuscule 2.9 percent. We're not saying that any market timer has ever been so far off the mark as to be out of stocks during all of their best days or months, but the record shows that timers do miss enough of those blastoff moments to hurt themselves badly.

So the conclusion is clear: *the risk of being out of the market when it's rising is much greater than the risk of being in it when it's falling.* In other words, you can't win the ball game if you're not on the field swinging at whatever the pitcher is serving up. Another reason this is true is that broadly speaking, the average market advance, over periods of months and years, is twice the magnitude of the average market decline.

As we've said, most triggering events that cause market shifts are unpredictable. It's true that at times markets will look obviously ripe for a big drop or a strong upsurge, because in the first case stock valuations are high and investors are ebullient and in the second case valuations are low and pessimism is rampant. But it's also true that markets often stay at such extremes for long periods and it takes some news that's "different" to shift attitudes and prices. For example, stocks had been dirt cheap all the way from 1977 to mid-1982, selling consistently below ten times earnings because of high inflation and sluggish earnings—and no one saw any end to that discouraging picture. Then, in mid-1982, it suddenly became apparent that inflation was really slowing and the market took off like a rocket, rising 35 percent in three months (and tenfold in the next sixteen years).

Conversely, in 1987 everything related to the economy and corporate profits looked rosy, so stock prices jumped an amazing 40 percent between New Year's Day and Labor Day. Six weeks later, interest rates unexpectedly rose toward 10 percent and Congress began to consider legislation that would have slowed the rapid pace of corporate acquisitions that had been under way. The result was a precipitous drop in stocks that was greatly exacerbated by several new types of computerized trading by professional investors. Neither those managers nor most other investors truly understood how those techniques would work in a declining market—until they contributed to the notorious 25 percent drop between Friday morning and Monday's close on October 29.

Then in 1990 another surprise—Iraq's invasion of Kuwait—hit the market, causing a 20 percent slump from its all-time high. Most embarrassed on that early August day when the tanks rolled south was the Wall Street oil analyst who had written a report the week before titled, "Iraq Will Not Invade Kuwait." Similarly, in the spring of 1997 investors were ga-ga about the great economic growth taking place in Asia and were buying Asian nations' stocks with wild enthusiasm. Then the Thai baht suddenly collapsed in June and, as they say, the rest is history.

So in looking for turning points in the market, all one can do is try to expect the unexpected, and understand that unanticipated events will always eventually turn around markets that are at extreme lows or highs in their valuation.

The final impediment to successful market timing—human psychology—is impossible to quantify, but it's very potent. It takes more courage than most people have to sell stocks when all the news is good, most investors are strongly optimistic, and the market is soaring. And it requires a huge amount of self-confidence to buy stocks when everything looks bad and gloom and fear are pervasive. Therefore, market timers usually take action well after turning points in the market occur, waiting for events to bolster their courage. These delays greatly reduce the benefits of moving in and out of stocks.

Thus, because of the three factors we've discussed, it's very hard to make good market timing decisions. Yet, two comprehensive academic studies—by Nobel laureate Professor William Sharpe in 1975 and by Professors Jess H. Chua and Richard S. Woodward in 1987—show that to beat a buy-and-hold stock strategy, the timer has to make correct buy and sell decisions *70 to 75 percent of the time.* That's virtually impossible, given all the variables and uncertainties in the investment equation. Moreover, the cost of making even one bad decision can be devastating. For example, an old friend who was an experienced professional investor thought the 35 percent rebound in the market between August and October 1982, was "too much" and sold half his stocks when the Dow Average hit 1200. The Dow never saw 1200 again and in the remaining seven years of his life my friend never put his cash back into stocks.

A final reason why market timing is counterproductive for individual investors is that selling in high markets incurs the sizable cost of capital gains taxes—and it is practically impossible to make the accurate decisions needed to offset that expense.

Understanding all this, two of the wisest investors of the twentieth century had these comments:

> BERNARD BARUCH: "Don't try to buy at the bottom and sell at the top. It can't be done except by liars."

> WARREN BUFFETT: "The only value of stock forecasters is to make fortune-tellers look good."

Bond Market Forecasting

It's worth noting that bond market forecasting is just as hazardous as predicting future swings in stock prices. In 1989, Robert Farrell, the very able stock market strategist for Merrill Lynch, compiled this summary of the interest rate forecasts of the several score "leading economists" who are surveyed every January and July by *The Wall Street Journal.*

Since these knowledgeable experts, as a group, were wrong ten times out of eleven, one could ask why *The Wall Street Journal* continues to publish these surveys. Looked at one way, however, they really do serve a useful purpose, because if we always assume that events will turn out exactly opposite to the economists' forecasts, we should be right most of the time!

Six-Month Interest Rate Moves

	Forecast	Actual	Outcome – Right	Outcome – Wrong
January 1984	Slight Drop	Rise		✓
July	Rise	Drop		✓
January 1985	Rise	Drop		✓
July	Slight Rise	Slight Drop		✓
January 1986	Slight Drop	Large Drop		✓
July	Stable	Slight Drop		✓
January 1987	Drop	Rise		✓
July	Stable	Large Rise, Then Large Drop		✓
January 1988	Drop	Slight Rise		✓
July	Rise	Rise	✓	
January 1989	Rise	Large Drop		✓

Chapter 13

WHEN TO BAIL OUT

Many investors make more costly mistakes when selling stocks than when buying. Yet selling plays a key role in a successful portfolio—even for disciplined investors who select their purchases with great care. So any investor should understand when to move out of a stock.

The first and most important reason for selling is that a company is not living up to expectations. Either because its fundamental circumstances have changed or because you misanalyzed its basic business characteristics at the outset, the company lacks the strengths and favorable *long-term* prospects you saw when you bought the stock.

This is easy to say, but hard to put into practice. Even the best companies encounter problems and disappointments occasionally. Since these usually prove to be temporary,

they are not a reason to sell the stock—but
their temporary nature may not always be
evident at the outset. This means the investor should not rush to judgment when a
hitherto strong company hits an air pocket.
Instead, you must analyze the situation
carefully to determine whether the problem
is likely to prove short-lived or long-lasting.
Such an evaluation can be very difficult, because we never have all the information we
need. Thus, even the most capable investors
make more mistakes answering the tempo-
rary/permanent question than any other. I
know I have.

You may feel pushed to sell the stock by
worry about its price decline and by the typical negative comments made by Wall Street
analysts—whose focus is always very short-
term—after any disappointment in one of
"their" companies. However, the sensible approach is to go back to the business fundamentals of the company and ask yourself
whether the quarterly earnings shortfall,
product difficulty, or whatever the problem
is, has truly diminished the competitive position of the company or whether the industry in which the company operates has
deteriorated. In doing this, try to assess
what has changed and what has not.

When dealing with strong, successful businesses, one should generally lean toward the

view that the problem will be worked out in a reasonable length of time—because, as we emphasized in earlier chapters, the basic characteristics of companies and industries usually persist for long periods, and at worst they normally change very slowly. But even if you reach that conclusion initially and decide to hold on, you must review the problem continually. Sometimes difficulties are *not* resolved and the stock involved will underperform for a long time.

Don't worry if you don't come up with a clear answer right away. It's better to take enough time to develop a fully reasoned conclusion, even if that means selling the stock after it's way down, than to decide quickly on the basis of limited, preliminary information and find you've sold at a very temporary low in the stock, because the cloud passes and the share price quickly rebounds.

Among professional investment managers these days, the tremendous pressure to achieve good short-term performance has created a shoot-from-the-hip mentality. Bail out now and ask questions later is their usual approach. For example, all those who dumped Cisco in February and March of 1997 because of an expected slowdown of earnings growth from over 50 percent to 30 percent for a quarter or two, driving the stock down 38 percent, cost their clients dearly when growth did not decelerate that much and the stock proceeded to double in the next nineteen months.

Similarly, those who worried in early and mid-1996 about a lull in new pharmaceuticals from Eli Lilly—ignoring the ongoing excellence of the company's large R&D program—got suckered out of the stock as it slipped 20 percent just before several promising new drugs came along and pushed it up 85 percent in seven months.

The second reason for selling a stock is that it gets grossly overvalued by all the yardsticks discussed in Chapter 7—that is, it becomes so popular that its price reflects far greater earnings growth than can likely be achieved. When that happens, a good case can be made for selling in *non-taxable* portfolios. However, the decision may be different for accounts that have to pay capital gains taxes. If you own a stock that has, for instance, quadrupled over its cost—as so many did by the late 1990s—the combined federal and state capital gains tax for a holding of over twelve months amounts to roughly 25 percent of the gain, or almost *20 percent of the selling price*. This means the stock has to fall more than 20 percent before you have "saved" anything.

Furthermore, if the company is really strong and well positioned for the future, presumably you would like to buy it back if the stock does fall and its valuation becomes more reasonable. But will you have the courage and conviction to repurchase after a sizable price drop? Unfortunately, people often don't get back in when they should. So you should sell really good stocks when they become demonstrably overvalued only after carefully weighing potential short-term advantages versus potential long-term risks.

Like a garden, every portfolio needs some weeding on a regular basis. The pace of this weeding should largely be determined by the emergence of attractive buying opportunities in high-grade stocks you don't currently own. If something looks really attractive, make room for it by selling an existing holding with less promising prospects—even if it is a "good" investment. This type of approach usually produces more switches during or after a general market decline, because more favorable buying opportunities are then available. In fact, the *only* time many top-drawer companies sell at really attractive valuation levels is during bear markets.

This was true of the best drug stocks during their special bear market in 1992 to 1993, when they fell 40 to 50 percent. A period of widespread opportunity for useful portfolio shifting occurred in 1990 when the

Iraqi invasion of Kuwait drove most stocks down well over 20 percent. Late that summer, it was possible to buy many blue chip companies at less than half the valuation levels that had prevailed earlier and did again after 1995. More recently, the market's slump in the second half of 1998 opened up another favorable period for buying great stocks at attractive prices.

Although waiting for good switch opportunities makes great sense, don't delay on kicking out a former peacock when it turns into a turkey. When selling, you will get substantial benefits from realizing losses in your taxable accounts. A tax loss is money in the bank because, if realized, it means writing smaller checks to the IRS and state revenue department on April 15. Therefore, individuals should capture all their losses (that amount to 10 percent or more) every year. Do this before late November, because heavy tax selling usually occurs near year end, further depressing the prices of stocks that haven't been doing well.

Looking at the various reasons for selling stocks, what is an appropriate turnover for a long-term portfolio that concentrates in high-grade stocks? Based on the experience of successful managers, it is approximately 10 to 15 percent per year. So in a list of thirty stocks, three or four would be replaced each year. Any more than that would indicate poor initial selection. And much less would prevent keeping the portfolio up-to-date.

For taxable accounts, turnover much above 10 percent creates an excessive capital gains tax burden that hurts the net performance of the account. This is well documented in a 1993 study by Robert H. Jeffrey and Robert D. Arnott. In a way, this restraint on selling imposed by capital gains taxes is helpful, because there is no evidence that high turnover helps portfolio performance. And high turnover is usually based on short-term considerations that take the investor's eye off the very important long-term ball. Investors who focus on high-grade companies and have long-term goals should heed the advice of Walter Bagehot, the wise editor of *The Economist* for many years: "Overactivity is a very great evil."

Chapter 14

NO NEED FOR WHITE KNUCKLES

Most investors find stock market declines as distressing as the scary turbulence they encounter every so often on airplane flights. But unless one must sell some stocks soon to raise cash for a particular expenditure, the best way to cope with a market slump is to "roll with the punch" and recognize two things:

1. Most declines end in a matter of months, just as a summer storm passes in a matter of minutes.

2. If you own the shares of strong companies with good long-term records, a decline will cause no deterioration in the quality of the portfolio or its ability to produce favorable returns in the future.

Considering the powerful uptrend in the stock market discussed in Chapters 2 and 12, it's not surprising that most market drops are rather brief (averaging just eight months) and that the market usually recoups the greater part of the declines in similarly short periods. This is shown by the following figures for all of the significant market drops since 1950, displayed in the table on p. 171.

Note that only two declines in the past half century lasted more than fourteen months—a very short period in the time frame of almost all investors. Those occurred in the late 1960s and early 1970s, when inflation soared to unprecedented rates owing to circumstances that are unlikely to be repeated in the future. Observe also that the average round trip from peak to trough and back to peak again has been only twenty-one months.

This doesn't mean that declines *seem* short when they're under way. Losing money, on paper at least, day after day and week after week isn't pleasant and it can seem like Chinese water torture while it's happening. But the key to dealing successfully with this is to own high-grade companies in which one can have great confidence.

For example, when General Electric's stock fell 35 percent in the autumn of 1987 and

STOCK MARKET DECLINES OF OVER 15 PERCENT: S&P 500, 1950 TO 1998

| | DECLINE | | MONTHS TO RECOVER* | |
| | | | 75% OF | 100% OF |
YEAR(S)	PERCENT	MONTHS	DECLINE	DECLINE
1953	15	9	4	6
1956–1957	16	6	3	5
1957	20	3	11	12
1961–1962	29	6	10	14
1966	22	9	5	6
1968–1970	37	18	9	22
1973–1974	48	21	20[†]	64
1975	15	2	2	4
1977–1978	18	14	1	6
1978	17	2	7	10
1980	22	2	3	4
1981–1982	22	13	2	3
1987	34	2	18[‡]	23
1990	20	3	5	5
1998	19	3	1	12
AVERAGE	24	8	7	12

* From market low.
[†] Fifty percent of decline recovered in five months.
[‡] Fifty percent of decline recovered in twelve months.

when Pfizer's shares dropped 28 percent in 1990, nothing had changed in the businesses of those companies. They were just as strong as ever and had just as favorable growth prospects as ever. All that had changed was investor attitude, and that had no impact on GE's and Pfizer's ability to increase their earnings, dividends, and fundamental values in the future. So investors who understood that basic truth did not worry too much about those market declines, and certainly they did not panic and dump the shares of GE and Pfizer after these stocks had slumped. Instead, they acted like owners of a business rather than owners of pesky, volatile stocks.

There's really no other way to cope with a bear market than drawing on experience. Once an investor has lived through one or two bad periods and seen that they were not the end of the world, it becomes much easier to retain one's equanimity and not worry too much. Furthermore, and this is very important, bear markets provide great opportunities for the sensible, forward-looking investor. In fact, *bear markets are the long-term investor's best friend*—because, as already noted, they create bargains in the high-quality stocks that are so frequently overpriced.

For example, in August 1990, blue chips like the following sold at or near their lowest price/earnings ratios in many years, and investors who bought them then have enjoyed superb results, as shown in the table on page 173.

PRICE/EARNINGS RATIOS

	1985 TO 1990 RANGE	AUGUST 1990	1998*	PRICE APPRECIATION, 1990 TO 1998 (%)
Automatic Data	29–15	15	33	473
General Electric	21–8	10	26	484
Illinois Tool Works	22–12	12	20	440
Hewlett-Packard	32–8	8	18	700
Merck	34–16	16	29	425
S&P 500	19–11	14	24	331

* October 1998.

The reverse side of stock market volatility—when prices surge upward—is rarely worrisome, but it can be dangerous. The risk during strong market advances is that investors may become overconfident and relax their valuation discipline when buying stocks, so they end up paying ridiculous prices even for high-quality issues. They also tend to relax their quality discipline, getting lured into risky "hot" issues at insane prices. These breakdowns of logic and common sense were widespread in 1997 and the first half of 1998, and they brought a lot of grief to those who succumbed.

So, "steady as she goes" is as good advice for the investor as it usually is for the helmsman of a ship.

Chapter 15

COMPETING
WITH THE GIANTS

Investing in stocks today is something like playing on a field with a horde of giants. Institutional investors have become so dominant in the daily activity of the market that they frequently overpower the trading process and cause rapid, large swings in prices far beyond what logic would indicate.

Though this is not a new phenomenon, it has been growing in intensity and it must be recognized and coped with by everyone making decisions to buy or sell stocks. The primary problem is that institutional investors tend to move swiftly in the same direction at the same time, trampling all the other investors who may be in their way.

The tremendous buildup of institutional assets started over three decades ago in the pension fund sector and gained further momentum in the 1990s with a flood of money into mutual funds. Thus, by 1998 the $14.5 trillion of total common stock outstanding was distributed as follows compared with twenty years earlier:

	1998 (%)	1978 (%)
Pension Funds	24	18
Mutual Funds	17	4
Insurance Companies	6	6
Foreign Investors	6	4
Security Dealers	1	1
TOTAL INSTITUTIONAL	54	33
INDIVIDUALS	46	67

Even this massive shift toward professionally managed portfolios understates the impact of institutions on the stock market, because they do much more buying and selling per dollar of assets than individuals do. For example, the annual turnover of mutual fund portfolios now approaches 100 percent. This means that, on average, each stock stays in the portfolio for just twelve months. Trading in pension funds is not quite so frenzied, but much more frequent than that of individuals.

The net result is that while institutions even now own just over half of all the stock outstanding, they dominate stock market activity, accounting for more than 80 percent of all the daily trading on the stock exchanges. And they move with the speed of electrons—literally. With modern communications networks disseminating news on the economy, all industries, and individual companies instantaneously throughout the professional investment community—and with institutional portfolio managers striving to produce superior results for clients who monitor their performance closely on a quarterly or even monthly basis—rapid decisions are made in response to new developments. Today's institutional trading rooms resemble battlefield command centers.

Because all institutional managers receive the same information at virtually the same moment, they often make buy and sell decisions simultaneously. These produce huge volume on one side of the market for the stocks involved, causing sharp price moves in a matter of minutes. Often the approach is, "I'll sell (or buy) now and figure out what this news means later." So the horde of giants goes stampeding into the market.

As a result, bad news can push down the stock of a big, strong company 10 to 15 percent in a matter of minutes, and good news can lift it a similar amount. In smaller, riskier companies, unexpected developments cause instantaneous moves of 25 percent or more, and there are some of these every day! This shows how firmly expectations get embedded in share prices and how stocks react when the anticipated does not occur.

Even in earlier times, when individuals dominated trading, the stock market experienced periods of high volatility—the late 1920s and late 1960s, for example. But now a different force—the growing impact of institutional investors who have a very short-term orientation—has made the stock market as bouncy as the mechanical bulls that used to be so popular in taverns across the country. So what should the individual investor do?

First, be aware that you are contending with a large number of giants who tend to charge off in the same direction much of the time. Second, pay close attention to the valuation of the stocks you own or are considering as purchases. If they are selling at or near their highs and have generous price/earnings ratios, chances are that institutional investors are large owners and maybe current buyers because they have optimistic expectations for those stocks. Any change in their attitudes will cause prices to tumble. The reverse applies, of course, to stocks with lower valuations, which reflect minimal expectations for the companies. Often, such issues are attractive because the big investors are not substantial owners and interested buyers. Patience may be required to reap the rewards from these stocks—but not being in a hurry is a desirable attitude for the true long-term investor. As Robert Farrell, Merrill Lynch's savvy market analyst, said in his October 8, 1984 report, "Only in the stock market do we plant acorns and expect to be sitting in the shade of a tall oak in a matter of weeks or months." We have to overcome that temptation.

Third, respect the power of the large institutional investors, but don't be intimidated by it. Their judgment is far from infallible and they make many mistakes. So take advantage of them by adopting contrary views when there are sensible reasons for doing so. This requires courage, but for people whose time horizon extends beyond tomorrow morning, it does pay off.

PART V

PLANNING THE RACE

Chapter 16

WHAT ARE YOU TRYING TO ACCOMPLISH?

Just as no sensible generals go into battle without determining their objectives, no intelligent person launches a new business venture without specific goals. This applies to starting an investment program as well.

Investment objectives must be based on each particular individual's or institution's financial needs, and it is crucial to spend considerable time analyzing those needs before determining the objectives. The primary financial needs of most families are first, accumulating enough money to pay for the increasingly expensive college education of their children and second, financing a comfortable retirement for themselves. These needs can be calculated in dollar terms quite accurately with the help of a competent financial planner, an investment advisor, or a computer software package designed for that purpose.

If people start saving and investing at an appropriate time to meet these needs—that is, early in their working lives—the investment program for each objective is long term: fifteen years or more for education funds and at least two decades to build an adequate retirement nest egg. The period during which the retirement fund is utilized—and therefore must be managed effectively—is usually another several decades. The same long-term focus applies to defined contribution retirement funds—401(k) and 403(b)—whose primary investment decisions are made by employees, not professional investment managers.

As people evaluate their retirement needs, they should keep in mind that they will probably live a lot longer than their parents or grandparents. It's hard to believe that when Social Security started in 1935 the typical American worker died just two years after retirement at age sixty-five. Now, as shown in the figures below, the average male retiree will live seventeen years after age sixty-five and the average female twenty-one years. And the hearty ones will live twenty-five to thirty years or longer!

AVERAGE LIFE EXPECTANCY (YEARS)

AGE	MALE	FEMALE
35	42	48
45	33	39
55	25	29
65	17	21
75	11	14
85	5	7

Source: Centers for Disease Control

On the institutional side, defined benefit pension funds have very long time frames to meet their specific, actuarially determined needs. Insurance companies and endowment funds also have extremely long-term goals, the latter being really perpetual ones.

So the needs and objectives of almost all investment portfolios stretch out over very long periods of time. *This is the most important factor to consider in setting investment strategy.* Truly, for most people investing is not a sprint, it's a marathon, and it has to be carried out with the kind of preparation, discipline, determination, and measured pace that successful long-distance runners are known for.

Another key factor in your investment planning is inflation. Way back when the currencies of the world were based on gold, inflation occurred only during wars—and when peace returned, a painful deflation quickly brought the cost of living back down to where it had been before the conflict. As a result, in 1931 the U.S. Consumer Price Index was only slightly higher than when George Washington was president!

But then the world went off the gold standard and the strict monetary discipline it had imposed disappeared. As a result, during the past half century the cost of living has risen every single year—in peacetime as well as wartime—at an average annual increase of a little over 3%.

As depicted in the chart below, inflation accelerated to much faster rates during the 1970s, reaching a peak of 13.5 percent in 1980. This was caused by several oil price shocks, sharp increases in the federal budget

ANNUAL INFLATION RATE
CONSUMER PRICE INDEX

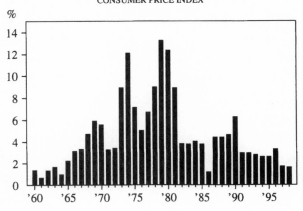

deficit (to finance both the Vietnam War and the new Great Society social programs), and a loose monetary policy that more than tripled the growth rate of the money supply, from 4 percent in 1960 to several peaks of 13 percent.

The conditions responsible for this wild inflation in the 1970s are unlikely to recur, for three primary reasons. First, intense worldwide competition has made it very difficult for most businesses to raise prices significantly, even when their costs go up. To maintain their profit margins, they must now improve efficiency, because their customers will not accept substantial price increases; they'll just take their business elsewhere, in the U.S. or overseas. This global competition is likely to persist as far ahead as anyone can see.

Second, the devastation caused by runaway inflation in the 1970s is so impressed on people's minds—whether they be business executives, government officials, politicians, or other citizens—that they will not let it recur. Widespread approval of the citizenry for a balanced federal budget is one indication of this.

Third, the U.S. government, along with every other government, has become very dependent on the bond market to buy the new issues it must sell for additional financing and to roll over its maturing debt. But if bond investors see any country's fiscal or monetary affairs getting out of control, they will refuse to buy that nation's bonds or will only do so at exorbitant interest rates.

This gives governments considerable incentive to avoid inflationary fiscal or monetary policies. The "bond market vigilantes" are always lurking in the shadows to rein in profligate governments—as are currency traders, whose selling will quickly drive down the currency of any nation that mismanages its financial affairs.

The bond market's continuing concern about inflation is clearly shown by the fact that during 1995 and early 1996 bond prices rose and fell precisely in line with the prospects that Congress and the president would agree on a realistic deficit reduction program.

The only event we can visualize now that would upset the inflation apple cart and start the Consumer Price Index rising rapidly again would be a disruption of oil supply from the Middle East. That area, with its turbulent politics, controls 60 percent of the world's oil reserves, and any reduction in the availability of Middle East oil would quickly spark a surge of inflation, as happened briefly after the Iraqis invaded Kuwait in 1990. Barring this possibility, we are not faced with the likelihood of double-digit or even high single-digit inflation in the foreseeable future. However, investors should factor in an annual inflation rate of at least 3 percent for long-term planning.

As the 1990s draw to a close at this writing, some people maintain that investors' concerns now shouldn't be inflation, but rather *deflation*. It is true that the Asian economic crisis has caused widespread price declines in all raw materials (oil, chemicals, paper, metals, etc.), agricultural products, and some manufactured goods where productive capacity had been built up too fast, causing surpluses. But although deflation has developed in one segment of the world economy, there are two good reasons to believe it probably won't spread to other sectors.

The most important reason is that in all the larger economies around the world, service activities—including the private and public sectors—are considerably larger than manufacturing (including extracting and processing the raw materials used to make goods). In 1998, total services accounted for 57 percent of the U.S. gross domestic product. This is significant because services, consisting mainly of personnel costs, are not subject to deflationary pressures except under extreme circumstances.

This leads to the second reason: the Federal Reserve and other central banks will move forcefully to counter full-scale deflation by boosting money supplies and lowering interest rates as they did in the autumn of 1998. The lesson of the 1930s, when the Fed did not take such action, has been well learned.

So, while nothing is impossible in the economic arena, the chances of widespread deflation in the years ahead seem quite small.

Inflation of 3 percent sounds like an inconsequential number, but the fact is that such a rate raises the cost of living substantially over any period of more than a few years—and a rate just 1 percent higher considerably worsens the problem.

THE IMPACT OF INFLATION

RISE IN COST OF LIVING	ANNUAL RATES	
	3%	4%
After: 5 Years	+16%	+21%
10	+34	+48
15	+56	+80
20	+81	+119
25	+111	+166
30	+143	+224
35	+181	+294
40	+226	+380
45	+278	+484

Observe that over the average life expectancy of close to twenty years for people reaching normal retirement age, the cost of living will rise 81 percent at a 3 percent inflation rate and 119 percent at the slightly faster pace of 4 percent. More important, by the time age sixty-five rolls around for a thirty-five-year-old worker who is just starting to save for retirement, the initial dollars put into his or her retirement fund will buy only one half to one third as much food or heating oil as they do today (if those dollars don't grow).

This may sound surprising to thirty-five-year-olds, but to most older people who are now retired, it's not. When *they* started work, ice cream cones cost a nickel, automobiles cost $850 and a good house was priced no higher than $25,000. So be prepared to pay $50,000 for an ordinary Chevy by the year 2020 and $100,000 around 2030.

For educational funds, the inflation problem is even more difficult because for many years tuition rates have been rising at twice the pace of the Consumer Price Index. This disparity results primarily from the fact that it is very hard to improve productivity in educational institutions if professor/student ratios stay constant.

The same inflation factors apply to most institutional portfolios. In the case of defined benefit pension plans, active workers' wage and salary rates tend to rise more or less in line with inflation and that translates directly into higher payments from the company's pension fund as each year's group of employees reaches retirement.

Inflation has a somewhat similar impact on loss payments by property/casualty insurers. And those companies also need to grow their capital so they can write more insurance as inflation pushes up the amount of coverage policyholders need.

To the extent that life insurance companies still write policies with fixed death payments, they are not impacted greatly by inflation. However, more and more of their products are aimed at protecting customers against inflation, so the investments for these products must be based on the certain uptrend in the cost of living.

Educational institutions have the greatest need for inflation protection in their endowment portfolios because of the very rapid rise in their annual costs, as just mentioned.

Once individuals or institutions determine the needs and objectives (in inflation-adjusted terms) of their investment program, they must analyze various types of investments to see which are appropriate, and in what mix. For starters, let's examine the relative merits of bonds versus stocks.

Chapter 17

COMFORT
VERSUS PROFITS

Bonds and stocks are the two primary forms of investment.

Real estate is an equity alternative to the common stock of corporations, but because most income-producing real estate consists of large properties, each worth millions of dollars, investing indirectly in such assets is practical only for large institutional portfolios. Even they often participate in pools of properties, sharing investments in specific buildings with other institutions.

Individuals, of course, can invest in real estate through equity real estate investment trusts (REITs). Shares of these trusts trade on the various stock exchanges and can be attractive for investors seeking generous current income and moderate growth.

Bond Comfort

As the debt obligations of a corporation or other borrower, bonds pay a fixed rate of income on a scheduled basis, usually every six months, until they mature. At that point investors receive a fixed dollar amount of capital—$1000 cash per $1000 face value of the bonds they hold. This makes most bonds very secure, and therefore comfortable investments for many people.

Both interest and principal repayments, of course, depend on the continued financial viability of the borrower. If the company goes bankrupt, investors may end up receiving less than was promised to them—or nothing. That is a rare occurrence, but even a moderate deterioration in a firm's financial condition can cause the prices of its bonds to decline.

U.S. Treasury obligations and, to a considerable extent, federal government agency issues, are not subject to such credit risk. Municipal bonds issued by states, cities, towns, and their agencies have some credit risk, although defaults are unusual. Their primary advantage is tax-exempt income.

Most bond issues of any significant size are assigned quality ratings by rating agencies, including Standard & Poor's and Moody's. The agencies evaluate factors related to financial strength and the risks inherent in the business or the type of government operation. The top-quality issues (notably U.S. Treasury bonds and notes) are rated AAA, while the gradations in "investment quality" issues go down to BBB (Baa in Moody's). Then, down through B and the Cs the quality ratings get progressively worse. This is the "junk bond"—or, more politely, "high-yield bond"—area.

Here are a few quotations from Moody's describing the bonds that rank below investment grade: Ba ("have speculative elements . . . future not well-assured"), B ("generally lack characteristics of desirable investment"), Caa ("of poor standing . . . may be in default or . . . present elements of danger"), Ca (speculative in a high degree . . . often in default"), C ("lowest rated . . . extremely poor prospects").

Overall, the average quality of noninvestment grade bonds has improved in recent years, so a well-managed portfolio of high-yield bonds can be appropriate for some investors. Individuals, however, should own such bonds only through a good mutual fund.

Nowadays, many municipal bonds are insured by specialized insurance companies (like MBIA Insurance Corp., Financial Guaranty Insurance Corp., Ambac Assurance Corp., and Financial Security Assurance Corp.), as are some corporate bonds sold to individual investors. This enhances their safety and gets them higher ratings by the agencies.

Beyond strength of credit, the other influence on bond prices is interest rates. When rates rise because of higher inflation, greater loan demand, a tighter monetary policy by the Federal Reserve, or some other factor, new bond issues come out at higher interest rates and the prices of those already outstanding drop, to provide the prevailing higher yields to new buyers of them. Most important, issues with longer maturity dates drop much more in price than shorter ones. When interest rates decline, the process is reversed and longer-term issues *rise* more in price.

Thus, long-term bonds have much greater price volatility. In the past decade we have seen price swings in thirty-year bonds of up to 25 to 30 percent in a single year, while issues of five years and shorter moved just a few percent. Therefore, "fixed-dollar assets" can be far from stable in the market, even though they keep paying their interest regularly.

This is illustrated by the following table, which shows how much the prices of five 6.00 percent bonds of equal quality but different maturities would decline if the market level of interest rates were to increase by half-percent increments up to 8.00 percent.

THE DOWNSIDE RISK IN BONDS: BY MATURITY—COUPON 6.00 PERCENT

	PRICE AT A YIELD OF:				
MATURITY	6.00%	6.50%	7.00%	7.50%	8.00%
2 Years	100	99	98	97	96
5	100	98	96	94	92
10	100	96	93	90	86
20	100	94	89	85	80
30	100	93	88	82	77

The maturity date of a bond is like a magnet, and the closer a particular issue is to when it will be paid off at 100 percent of its par value, the more power the magnet has to hold the bond up in a declining market. When interest rates drop, the process is reversed and longer-term issues rise more.

Bonds have become more volatile in the past several decades than they used to be in the good old days, but their prices generally fluctuate much less than those of stocks and they almost always pay off at par when they mature. Also, their income is quite reliable—so, if properly chosen, they are a good source of stability in an investor's portfolio. Furthermore, because they have much less potential for long-term capital gains (even when bought in a depressed market), bonds provide a higher current income than most stocks, an attraction for some types of investors.

To take advantage of the lower price volatility bonds can provide, and to avoid having to guess the future shifts in interest rates, it is usually desirable for individual investors to "ladder" the maturities of the bonds they own, having one or more issues coming due every year or so, out to a maximum of ten to twelve years.

Many bond issues (not including U.S. Treasuries) contain "call" features. This means that the company or municipality issuing the bond can call it for early redemption—often many years before the stated maturity—at par or a few points above par. This is a real disadvantage for the investor, because the issuer will call the bond only if interest rates have declined, making it possible to pay off the outstanding bonds and replace them with a new issue carrying a lower interest rate. So the investor will lose income by having to reinvest the proceeds from the call at a lower rate of interest.

Conversely, if interest rates rise, the issuer is happy to have the original bonds remain outstanding, because calling them would require selling new bonds at higher rates. Therefore, generally speaking, callable bonds are a "heads-I-lose, tails-you-win" proposition for investors.

Institutions, with their greater knowledge and their ability to trade bonds actively, can invest successfully in callable issues and take advantage of the slightly higher current yields they typically offer over noncallable bonds. But this is not a game for the amateur, because it does have risks. For example, huge numbers of bonds issued in the high-interest-rate environment of the 1970s and 1980s have been called for early redemption in the 1990s, a very negative development for their owners.

As will be shown shortly, over the years intermediate-term bonds (seven- to ten-year maturities) have provided slightly higher returns than long-term bonds, and have experienced only about two-thirds as much price volatility. So for most investors it isn't worthwhile to assume the additional price risk of owning long-term bonds.

Stock Profits

Common stocks are governed mostly by different factors. The financial strength of a company is important for its stock, but more significant is its ability to grow—to achieve higher sales, profits, and dividends. As we have emphasized, *in the long run, the price of a stock is determined by the trend of earnings per share and dividends per share.* The more these grow, the more the stock will ultimately be worth. This is the basic fact of equity investing.

In the shorter run, though, the shares of even the companies having the highest quality and the most successful growth can fluctuate widely in price as the general mood of investors swings between optimism and pessimism. The unpredictability of those shifts in mood explains why the course of the stock market from day to day, from week to week, and even from one year to the next is unpredictable. *Psychology rules in the short run and business fundamentals govern the long run.*

Many market "gurus" try to forecast what the market will do, but their long-term record of accuracy is mediocre at best—and often they make bad mistakes at crucial turning points. A favorite example is the market analyst of a major brokerage firm who said in early August 1982 that "the summer rally is over"—just two days before the greatest bull market in history started (when the Dow Jones Industrial Average was 790).

The different characteristics of bonds and stocks are reflected in the returns they have provided to investors over the years. We have good records on securities prices, and their interest and dividend payments, going back over a century. Particularly detailed is the data compiled by Ibbotson Associates from 1926 on, which shows the following total returns (income and price appreciation combined, before taxes) for the seventy-three-year period through 1998.

ANNUAL AVERAGE TOTAL RETURNS 1926–1998

Small Stocks	12.4%
Large Stocks	11.2
Long-Term Corporate Bonds	5.8
Long-Term Government Bonds	5.3
Intermediate-Term Government Bonds	5.3
Treasury Bills	3.8
Inflation	3.1

Source: Ibbotson Associates

Observe that the securities with higher interim price risks have provided higher returns, except for the minor differential between long-term and intermediate-term government bonds. So the markets function in a logical fashion.

However, investors shouldn't carry that to an extreme and invest all their money in the riskiest stocks in order to maximize their returns. They will have a wild roller-coaster ride along the way that may well scare them into doing the wrong thing at the wrong time—and if they end up as one of the below-average achievers in that category, they will incur devastating losses.

This leads to the question of volatility: the degree of price swings in different types of bonds and stocks and the variability of their returns in different time periods. Here is the record over the past seventy-three years as measured by standard deviation.

STANDARD DEVIATION OF RETURNS, 1926–1998

Small Company Stocks	33.8%
Large Company Stocks	20.3
Long-Term Government Bonds	9.2
Long-Term Corporate Bonds	8.6
Intermediate-Term Government Bonds	5.7
U.S. Treasury Bills	3.2

Source: Ibbotson Associates

Standard deviation is a measure of the variation around an average or mean. For investments, it measures volatility, or risk. For example, in two thirds of the years since 1925, the total returns on stocks have ranged between 20.3 percent above their long-term mean (average) and 20.3 percent below. For long-term government bonds, the range two thirds of the time has been plus or minus 9.2 percent.

The much higher standard deviations of returns on stocks than on bonds lead some investors to believe that stocks are very risky. For anyone with a long-term investment horizon who is dealing with high-quality stocks, that is an erroneous conclusion. It is true that stock prices can fluctuate widely in fairly short periods, sometimes falling sharply and at other times rising rapidly. But, as discussed in previous chapters, the *long-term trend* of stock prices is strongly upward and usually market declines are relatively brief periods (in any sort of long-term context). This means the much higher average annual returns on stocks than on bonds far more than make up for stocks' greater short-term price volatility. So investors whose objectives are measured in decades rather than years are well rewarded for the extra "risk" they take in owning stocks. And there is a real price over the long term—in passed-up returns— for the comfort bonds provide.

Chapter 18

BALANCING THE ALTERNATIVES

It's now time to take up the critical issue of *asset allocation:* determining the ratio of bonds to stocks in a portfolio and the type of stocks most suitable for your needs and goals.

In setting the equity ratio, there are three primary considerations: (1) your time frame, (2) your relative need to build capital and future income versus producing a certain level of current income, and (3) your "risk tolerance"—that is, your ability to cope with the occasional sharp declines the stock market undergoes, without becoming unduly fearful or panicky near the low and selling out.

The first market decline a person experiences with significant dollars personally at stake is always the toughest. Seeing your stocks eventually recover and move on to new highs proves that the bite of the bear is not life-threatening, but you have to experience that directly to fully believe it. In fact, as I have already said, bear markets are really the long-term investor's best friend— because that's when the best opportunities become available for buying stocks at cheap prices and upgrading even an already good portfolio.

Investors do have to decide, however, how important it is for them personally to dampen the price volatility of their particular portfolios with bond ownership so they can sleep reasonably well at night during the very discouraging and sometimes scary bear markets that usually occur at least once a decade. The table on page 207 illustrates the cost, in long-term returns, of moderating declines in portfolio values during bear markets. It shows what would happen to a starting portfolio of $1 million with various stock/bond ratios during a 25 percent drop in the stock market accompanied by an increase of 1.00 percent in interest rates on intermediate-term bonds—and what the twenty-year growth in the value of these portfolios would be, based on a conservatively estimated annual return of 10.5 percent for large company stocks and recent years' interest return of 6.00 percent on intermediate-term U.S. Treasury bonds.

BEAR MARKET PROTECTION
vs. LONG-TERM GAINS

Starting Portfolio: $1 Million
Long-Term Returns: Stocks 10.5% Annually, Bonds 6.0%

STOCK/BOND RATIO:	50/50	60/40	70/30	80/20	90/10	100/0
Portfolio's Decline in Market Value If Stocks Drop 25% and Intermediate-term Bonds Drop 4%	−14.0%	−16.6%	−18.7%	−20.8%	−22.9%	−25.0%
Total Value at Low ($000)	$860	$834	$813	$792	$771	$750
Advantage vs. 100/0 Portfolio	15%	11%	8%	6%	3%	
Long-Term Values after 20 Years ($000)	5289	5703	6118	6534	6950	7366
Advantage vs. 50/50 Portfolio		8%	16%	24%	31%	39%

Obviously, over the long run the "insurance premium" of a low stock ratio is fairly expensive. Taking the two extremes, the 50/50 investor will have 15 percent more capital at the bottom of the bear market than the courageous investor who puts all his or her money in stocks. But in twenty years—the average life span of a retiree—the latter will have 39 percent more capital. And if the long-term time frame is extended to forty years—the actuarial life span of today's thirty-seven-year old investor—the ultimate advantage of being 100 percent in stocks jumps to 67 percent.

In reality, most people prefer at least some anchor to windward in their portfolios during bear markets, so even individual investors who have great confidence in the long-term potential for stocks often like to have 20 to 30 percent of their portfolios in bonds. The foregoing figures show that's plenty of protection, perhaps too much.

On the institutional side, endowment funds, which at least theoretically have the longest time horizon (forever), typically hold 65 to 70 percent of their assets in stocks and equity real estate, while defined benefit pension funds average near 60 percent.

In the late 1990s, with the dividend yields on stocks well under 2 percent (vs. their post-World War II average of 4.3 percent), people who require a reasonable amount of income to pay their current living expenses have felt a need to own more bonds and fewer stocks. However, it is not a good idea for those with a life expectancy of more than ten years to cut their stock ratio down much below 60 percent. They would be better off maintaining the inflation protection of a substantial stock ratio and spending a little of the accumulated capital appreciation on their stocks each year.

Based on the expectation that the historical total return on stocks of 11 percent and the historical inflation rate of 3 percent will persist beyond the coming decade, the investor with 60 to 65 percent of his or her portfolio in stocks can afford to cash out enough capital gains each year to spend 4.5 to 5.0 percent of the portfolio's total market value and still keep up with inflation. This is the typical spending policy of endowment funds in the late 1990s—based on their sophisticated analyses of long-term returns and risks.

In the end, every individual investor and every professional manager has to keep asset allocation at a level he or she will be comfortable with through thick and thin. Once that allocation is determined, it is essential to stick to it—because the tendency to modify bond and stock ratios is always greatest at extremes in the market, when almost inevitably any shift will be made in the wrong direction. For example, after the really scary 35 percent drop in the market during just five days in October 1987, many investors decided to lower their stock ratios—just when stocks were the cheapest they had been in three years and when price/earnings ratios were 25 percent below their long-term average. A decade later, when P/Es had risen some 75 percent, to the top of their long-term range, desired stock ratios had moved up to near all-time highs. This, of course, defies the common sense that is so important for long-term investment success.

Chapter 19

WHY SQUIRRELS AND EARLY BIRDS EAT WELL

Squirrels gather nuts diligently all fall and store them in safe places, so they are never hungry in the winter. Investors who do the same prosper mightily. And the ones who do particularly well are those who start the process long before their financial needs become compelling. The early bird gets lots of juicy worms in the stock market.

If people or institutions really want to build capital and income for the future, they should do more than just strive for good investment performance. As soon as possible, they should also start saving at least some of their current income every year and investing it in good stocks. Three examples illustrate the great benefits of socking away money early and often.

The first is an individual who became a client of our firm in 1960. At the time, he had a stock portfolio worth about $200,000, which he had accumulated from several modest inheritances. His salary then was rather moderate, and it only grew gradually to about $85,000 by the time he retired in 1990. But during those 30 years, he continually saved money and we invested it for him in high-grade growth stocks. The higher his salary rose, the more he saved. By 1998, his portfolio was worth $7 million.

Another client, a small privately owned company that has had uneven profits, has regularly paid the maximum allowable amounts into its defined benefit pension fund and profit-sharing trust—even at the expense of squeezing salaries in lean years. Result: the firm's older employees have been retiring in recent years with retirement funds of $1 million to $3 million apiece to roll over into their IRA accounts.

The final striking example is Harvard University—which has by far the largest endowment fund of any educational institution, now worth $13 billion. A significant portion of that value has come from the policies established by Paul C. Cabot, Harvard's treasurer from 1948 to 1965. Cabot cofounded and for many years was the lead partner in State Street Research & Management Co., a very successful investment management firm in Boston. He was a strong believer in common stocks in the early years after World War II, when most investors were cool toward equities because of their very poor performance during the 1930s and early 1940s. Cabot's first move as Harvard's treasurer was to sell many of the endowment fund's bonds and buy stocks. In 1948, the Dow Jones Average was around 180 and stocks were almost as cheap as they had ever been, selling at 7½ times earnings and yielding over 6 percent. The second step Cabot took was to establish a still ongoing policy of reinvesting a portion of each year's income in additional stocks. Based on the tremendous power of compounding, these two simple but very sensible decisions have added hugely to Harvard's wealth. In fact, based on my most conservative estimates, I believe the additional percentage that Cabot invested in stocks and the yearly income that was saved and reinvested are responsible for *at least $2 billion* of the Harvard endowment's present $13 billion market value!

Few of us can do that well as early birds and squirrels, because we're not starting with a fund of $200 million as Harvard was in 1948. But the game is worth playing to the full. As these three examples show, both institutions and individuals can benefit greatly from disciplined savings programs. And when the money set aside is invested in stocks, the old aphorism, "A penny saved is a penny earned," is wrong. A penny saved becomes many pennies earned. This is equally true for early birds like Harvard half a century ago or the individual who starts saving at age 30.

VALUE OF $1 AT AGE 65,
IF INVESTED TO EARN 10 PERCENT YEARLY

Starting Age:	30	35	40	45	50	55
Age 65 Value:	$28.10	$17.45	$10.83	$6.28	$4.18	$2.59

The conclusion is obvious: *Time is a huge ally of the investor.* There is further striking evidence of this in the runaway bestseller, *The Millionaire Next Door,* published in 1996 and a million copies later still selling briskly at this writing. The surveys on which this book is based show that most millionaire families got there for three more or less equal reasons: being successful in a business (often a small, unglamorous one); saving an average of nearly 20 percent of their annual after-tax income *every year;* and investing much of their savings in stocks. These people have followed very successfully the old adage, "Don't wait for your ship to come in; row out to meet it."

PART VI

PUTTING IT ALL TOGETHER

Chapter 20

BUILDING AN
EQUITY PORTFOLIO

Because an equity portfolio is so crucial to most people's long-run financial survival, it must be built with great care. And the verb *build* is most appropriate here, since a sturdy, lasting structure is needed to provide the capital and income required for a comfortable living over several decades or longer.

As with building a house, the first step is to determine what your investment needs will be (as discussed in Chapter 16). Similarly, your next step is to draw up a plan: how much money to put into stocks, over what time frame, and what kind of stocks to buy. The plan is crucial. You should follow it closely and review it regularly to make sure it is still appropriate. Your final step, of course, is to invest in companies that fit the requirements of your plan—when their shares can be bought at realistic valuations.

Depending on the general level of valuations in the market, the initial purchase process may be rapid or slow. If valuations are high, a gradual accumulation process makes sense. Called *dollar averaging,* this involves buying just half or one third of the desired ultimate positions in various stocks, and then buying more shares if prices drop— or even if they stay flat while the companies' earnings and dividends continue to grow. The advantage of dollar averaging is that it protects against the risk that a stock might drop sharply if temporary bad news hits it or the overall market slumps. Then it would have been a poor decision to have acquired a complete position before the drop.

The risk of gradual accumulation, of course, is that following its long-term uptrend a stock or the overall market will keep advancing and the investor won't have bought enough of what turns out to be an excellent investment. That is always a possibility, but there are lots of good companies to invest in and you don't have to own every one of them to do well. Many people who missed the boat in Coca-Cola, Microsoft, and Pfizer still have done well, because they owned Cisco, Colgate, and Merck.

A good approach in building a portfolio is to set general targets for diversification among the most attractive industry sectors and identify the strongest companies in those areas as good candidates to buy. Then, start purchasing the best values among those candidates, while continually looking for alternatives that would meet the portfolio's quality and valuation criteria.

Beginning with all cash, even in a high market, you should invest half the money in six months or less, because the market may keep on rising—as it did to many investors' surprise in the mid-1990s. Remember, being out of the market with much of your money means making a bet against a very powerful, very certain uptrend.

Normally, most of the cash should be committed to stocks within nine to twelve months—and certainly sooner if values are reasonable. This may mean not reaching the "ideal" diversification set out in the initial plan, but most likely there will be plenty of chances to work toward that later, since no group of stocks stays highly valued forever.

In stock markets where valuations are generally high, a good tactic in building a portfolio is to wait patiently for "fallen angels" to appear—which they will fairly frequently. These are stocks of good companies that encounter disappointing earnings, a new product that doesn't meet expectations, or some other problem that shows every sign of being just a temporary setback, not a fundamental weakening of the company. The bad news will dampen investor enthusiasm and cause the stock to fall, making it a much better value. This has happened frequently during the great bull market of the 1990s, and investors who have built their portfolios by patiently waiting for fallen angels have been able to accumulate excellent, well-diversified lists of top-drawer companies. All it takes is clearly knowing what you want to do and strictly following your plan without succumbing to the siren song of hot stocks like Internet issues, biotech stocks, or whatever.

Once you build your portfolio, your job is more than pure maintenance. A list of stocks must be kept up-to-date by weeding out companies that lose their momentum for any of a variety of reasons and introducing ones in promising new areas—such as computer software and services, which emerged in the early 1990s, and networking, which gained prominence in the mid-1990s. Every portfolio can be improved over time; if it isn't, it won't achieve your financial goals.

Chapter 21

PICKING A PRO

M any people fortunate enough to possess some capital or able to accumulate it are keenly interested in the investment process and have the innate ability to manage their own holdings. For such people, the obvious question is: why should I seek the services of a professional investment advisor?

The answer is simple. Advisors can provide what most individual investors just don't have: unlimited time, adequate information, lots of accumulated experience, and the objectivity that enables them to follow a disciplined program. Advisors have staffs of investment professionals who can devote full time to studying the general economy, various industries, a large number of companies, and security values—and they have acquired a great deal of knowledge on those subjects. Professional advisors, therefore, are better equipped to cope with the horde of giants discussed in Chapter 15.

This doesn't mean, of course, that they *always* make the right decisions. But advisors do have advantages over part-time investors who must settle for more superficial analysis or base their conclusions on the work of others whose capabilities they may not be able to judge.

Today's investment world—which is really the world of politics, law, economics, and businesses—is more complex than ever. It is also much riskier than it has been for many years, and it changes more rapidly. With all the unexpected gyrations we've experienced in stock prices during the past fifteen years, the process of picking good stocks and building a successful portfolio has become far more difficult. The key task of the investor, of course, is to make sound *long-term* judgments based on fundamental factors and objective valuation criteria—and even the investor who uses professional advice has to understand and monitor the process.

There are five major sources you can turn to for professional help. The most widely available is *bank trust departments*. Many banks offer investment management services, and some do a good job. Most, however, have to cope with the problems of trust officer turnover and large numbers of customers per officer. Unless you have really substantial assets, you are likely to be a small fish in a big pond with any of the larger banks. That makes it difficult to get effective personal service and build the kind of close understanding that is so important for a successful advisory relationship. In fact, in their efforts to maximize profits many banks today put even accounts worth up to several million dollars into pooled funds, thereby providing no personal investment service whatever. Just as the salesman in *The Music Man* said, "You have to know the territory," the investment advisor has to know his or her clients.

Brokers can be good sources of investment advice *if* their investment banking activities are not a major source of profits. That's a big if because, as described in Chapter 6, just about all the large firms earn much more from underwriting new issues than they do from helping investors to buy good stocks at good prices. In such firms, analysts are far more interested in maintaining friendly relationships with the companies they study in order to generate highly profitable underwriting business than they are in publishing truly objective opinions on those companies' stocks. This is why a mid-1998 study by The First Call Corporation, a research firm that tracks Wall Street analysts' opinions of 6000 stocks, found that more than a third were rated "strong buys," nearly a third "buys," roughly 30 percent "holds," and only 1 percent "sells." That in a market which had the highest valuations in history!

If you wish to use a broker for investment advice, be sure to seek a firm whose opinions are not tainted by the investment banking conflict. There are some brokers that meet that criterion, and they can do a good job for you. Also, even in the large firms there are individual brokers who help select investment counselors for customers seeking serious long-term portfolio management. This frees the broker to concentrate on making good executions of the purchase and sale orders initiated by the professional advisor, who is more objective.

Investment letters are another source of ideas. By their nature, though, they are impersonal and cannot do much to help an individual in planning an investment program to meet his or her particular needs and objectives. The founder of my old firm, David L. Babson, often likened the process of using investment letters to manage an investment portfolio to taking care of one's health by subscribing to the *Journal of the American Medical Association.*

Mutual funds are the ideal source of professional management for individuals with modest amounts of capital. A firm that runs one or more substantial mutual funds puts a strong effort into that activity because the funds are among its most important accounts—if not its only accounts. Furthermore, mutual funds provide much better investment diversification for individuals than they can achieve on their own with smaller amounts of capital. Even individual investors with sizable capital should use mutual funds for investing in international markets and small companies. In both those areas, diversification and specialized management skills are required—and they can only be obtained in very large, professionally managed portfolios, which means mutual funds for all but the biggest investors.

Millions of individuals are now invested in mutual funds, whether they want to be or not, via their employers' defined contribution pension plans—401(k) and 403(b) plans. This means they have to make selections among the various funds offered. How to choose mutual funds is beyond the scope of this book, but the general principles about equity investing recommended here also apply to funds. First, one must make an appropriate asset allocation decision: stocks versus bonds. Second, be sure to select funds with sensible investment strategies, based on quality and valuation, that have proven successful over the long term. Hot funds don't work any better than hot stocks, as noted in Chapter 8. Therefore, a fund's long-term record is generally the best indicator of its likely future performance—assuming, of course, that the same manager or management team is still in place.

Investment counselors are set up to provide comprehensive, objective, continuous advice on a personal basis. Since their fees are based on the market values of their clients' accounts, they are strongly motivated to manage portfolios well. As with mutual funds, long-term record plus continuity of investment philosophy and management personnel are key to judging the relative merits of different investment counseling firms.

Investment counselors provide the maximum personal service. Each client's needs and circumstances are handled individually—it's like buying custom-made suits, not ready-mades off the rack. For investors in the million-dollar-plus range, this can be very valuable.

What to Look For

Whatever type of advisor you seek, there are several important attributes to look for.

First, look for an *established, experienced firm*—a group of people who have accumulated considerable knowledge covering the whole range of investment climates and events.

Second, look for a firm with a *clearly defined investment philosophy* that is followed with great discipline. Some managers flit from one approach to another in a constant scramble always to be in tune with the market trend of the moment; but they too often end up being half a step behind or half a step ahead of the next shift in investor psychology. The result is poor performance.

Every successful investment manager has a sensible, logical investment approach and sticks to it. When golfers are off their game, they try hard to get back into the groove, to get swinging again in the way they have successfully in the past. Even investment managers who stay in the groove won't have superior results every year, because sometimes the market will be going against them, but when the market starts going their way again, they'll be right there at the outset.

It's most important to find an advisor who takes a *truly professional approach*—one who puts the interests of the client first, and is independent and free of conflicts. This is particularly important if you're considering a brokerage firm, because all but a few are rife with conflicts.

To be successful, a professional advisor must have *adequate resources* to do the job, including good analytical information, strong computer capability, and a realistic number of clients per portfolio manager. Some advisors work alone, but in today's complex investment environment it's extremely difficult for the solo advisor to succeed.

Effective *two-way communication* with clients is essential. The counselor has to know the client well and the client has to understand completely what the counselor is doing.

An advisor competent in *personal financial planning* is most desirable, because investments are only part of an individual's overall financial situation. The advisor's job is to fit the pieces together properly.

It almost goes without saying that the investment firm should be *strong financially*. You don't want an advisor who is cutting corners to keep the organization afloat.

As with mutual funds, make sure that the investment manager has had a *favorable long-term record*.

Now that institutional business has become so important and so lucrative, individual investors should also make certain that any advisor they pick has a *commitment to managing personal accounts as well as institutional ones*.

Don't pick an advisor because of low *fees*. That doesn't mean you should look for the professional with the highest rates, either—but all the other factors I have mentioned are more important than fees.

In evaluating a professional investment advisor, try to *talk to some of the advisor's existing clients* to get a first-hand appraisal of the firm. Satisfied clients are the best recommendation you can get.

Once you have selected an advisor, there are several ways in which you can make the relationship a productive one.

Your most important responsibility as a client is to help *establish a good understanding* between yourself and your advisor. You should carefully analyze your needs and objectives, communicate what they are, and be ready to modify them if the advisor's questions change your perceptions. At the outset, learn all you can about the advisor's investment philosophy. Once the two of you have developed a good understanding, your advisor can formulate a specific investment program to submit to you for approval.

To implement the program effectively, you should give your professional advisor (other than a broker) *discretionary power* to make purchases and sales without getting your prior approval for each transaction. To make this process work, you should set up simple, efficient mechanics, including a custodian arrangement with a bank or a financially strong brokerage firm. Some people become concerned that such a discretionary arrangement means turning over control of their investments to their advisor. That's not the case at all if you and the advisor work out a well-defined, detailed program in advance and you give it your stamp of approval. Moreover, exercising veto power over a professional advisor's individual purchase and sale decisions makes about as much sense as trying to tell your doctor whether to prescribe Lipitor or Pravachol to control your cholesterol. This doesn't mean you shouldn't follow with interest what your advisor is doing—but you should focus on whether the overall program is being implemented as you understood it would be. The advisor is responsible for notifying you promptly about every purchase and sale and describing briefly the reasons for each move.

Most successful investors are patient; they take a *long-term point of view.* So you should evaluate the performance of your advisor over a full market cycle. By that, I mean the full swing of the cycle for the advisor's particular investment approach, not necessarily just one complete swing in the Dow Jones Industrial Average. As I said earlier, no particular style works well in the market all the time. To maintain a portfolio of investments for many years, you want to run a successful marathon rather than try to win a series of sprints.

Should your financial circumstances change, or if you think they may, tell your advisor early on. Then, at the appropriate time the two of you can *redefine your needs and objectives* and alter your program to fit the new goals.

Finally, some advice that is especially important in exuberant bull markets: if you like to get some thrills in the stock market, you don't have to stifle that urge totally. Instead, set aside a separate "mad money" fund and play with it as hard as you want—but *don't mix it with your primary portfolio,* which is managed by your advisor.

Selecting and living with an investment advisor is something like getting married—it's not a step to be taken lightly. But if handled well and accompanied by a reasonable degree of good luck, it can lead to long years of happiness—for both parties.

Chapter 22

WHAT IT TAKES
TO WIN

Investors who do well in stocks differ from
each other in many ways—but they do
share a number of common characteristics.
Generally, these are not attributes one has
to be born with—so everyone can emulate,
to a substantial degree if they try hard
enough, the way the Warren Buffetts and
Peter Lynches operate.

• First, every successful investor I've ever
known or read about *has a very clear sense of
direction.* He or she has definite goals and a
precise investment strategy. This includes
delineating exactly the kind of stocks to be
owned and the valuation methods to be used.

• Second, these investors *follow their
plan and its particular strategy with great
discipline.* They don't deviate from their set
course for any reason. In fact, they follow
the approach of Admiral David Farragut in

the Civil War battle of Mobile Bay, where he gave his famous order, "Damn the torpedoes, full speed ahead." One of the most successful investors I have known sometimes waited five years or longer to buy companies he really wanted to own—because he had definite valuation limits and he knew that if he paid above those limits his returns could turn out to be unsatisfactory.

• This brings up the next attribute: *patience.* The stock market often moves up and down rapidly, as news comes out and investor attitudes change. Few activities are as subject to emotion as investing in stocks, and emotion is the enemy of rationality. So the investor who can stay calm and *logically* weigh the key factors involved in buy, sell, and hold decisions gains a great advantage. Patient investors don't chase rapidly rising stocks that have exceeded their valuation limits, nor do they often sell good stocks that have fallen to cheap prices. Fears about missing the boat lead to bad decisions. Usually the boat will come back again—and if it doesn't, another one will come along. Paraphrasing an old French proverb: patience can be bitter, but its fruit is sweet.

• Investors with good records invariably *look at things in perspective.* A snapshot of the present is interesting, but it has little meaning unless compared with past patterns and, if adequate long-term indicators are available, related to a reasoned judgment about the future. Obviously, experienced investors who have been analyzing businesses and managing portfolios for many years have lots of historical perspective in their heads. But they must use it!

Newer investors lack the perspective that experience provides, but they can gain it by studying the past (in general and related to specific industries and companies), talking with older investors, reading the many good books about or by experienced investors like Warren Buffett, Peter Lynch, David Dreman, and Ralph Wanger, and seeking out information that will help them assess the future.

During market extremes—the exuberant bull markets and the gloomy, scary bear markets—perspective pays off in spades because it shows investors that those *are* extremes, not something normal that will continue indefinitely. To illustrate the value of perspective, in 1994 to 1995 the personal computer industry was booming and, as a result, the semiconductor business was in its biggest boom ever. One of the hottest stocks was Micron Technologies, a leading U.S. producer of memory chips. By mid-1995, in just twelve months, Micron's earnings had jumped 440 percent and its stock had soared 850 percent. Not surprisingly, one of the large and very aggressive technology mutual funds had a big stake in Micron. In fact, it was the fund's largest position, accounting for 7 percent of total assets.

Apparently, the manager of the fund, who was then thirty-one years old and had been in the investment business for under eight years, hadn't spent much time studying the history of the semiconductor industry—especially DRAM memory chips, a feast-or-famine business for many years. Nor is it likely that he had studied the financial record of Micron very closely and seen that the company had operated at a deficit or breakeven in six of the previous ten years, or that its 1994 return on equity (ROE) of 29 percent was nearly triple its average ROE in the prior half dozen years. And he probably had not noticed the intense foreign competition in DRAM chips that had been building up for years.

Whatever he may or may not have done, it's hard to understand how any fund manager looking at Micron in perspective would have made it such a huge holding. But chances are this manager did question his aggressive purchase decision when the memory chip business suddenly entered one of its periodic slumps during the late spring and summer of 1996, causing Micron's earnings to plummet 82 percent in just six months and driving the stock down an equal 82 percent.

• The next important attribute of successful investors is that they *focus on companies, not stocks.* Analyzing and understanding companies isn't always easy, but there is plenty of factual information available that can help, and as pointed out earlier, the fundamental characteristics of businesses change only very slowly. That means it's much easier to appraise companies and forecast their likely future trends (not quarterly earnings, but basic longer-term trends) than it is to evaluate stocks and assess their possible moves over coming periods of weeks, months, and even several years. The unpredictable emotional factor makes the future course of stocks totally unpredictable except over very long periods—time spans that are not too long for true investors, but are far too long for those striving to achieve superior performance this month and this quarter.

A focus on companies not only enables investors to make much better-reasoned decisions; it also helps them keep calm during market extremes. Being able to worry less can make investing fun rather than a headache. And staying off the emotional roller coaster of the stock market prevents rash, stupid decisions.

Years ago, my firm had a client who was a nice man and a very successful insurance agent. But, despite all our efforts to concentrate his attention on the wonderful companies we had bought for him, the client was truly manic-depressive about the stock market. Every slump in stocks was agonizing for him, even though we tried to tell him that nothing had gone sour in Coca-Cola, GE, Merck, and the rest. Not surprisingly, he had a bad time in bear markets. But in a perverse way, he was some help to us—because, with remarkable precision, he telephoned us just days (honestly!) before the market lows in 1966, 1970, and 1974 and asked us to sell all his stocks. On each occasion, we talked him out of it, but he gave us great signals on the low points, spurring us to buy even more aggressively. I thanked him, but felt very sorry for his agony.

By contrast, on Black Monday of October 1987, when stocks were in free fall (dropping 20 percent that day!), 95 percent of the clients who telephoned me and my partners didn't want to sell anything; instead they asked whether they should *buy* more stocks. Their reasoning, which we had fostered over many years, was that nothing had really changed in the businesses of Air Products, Hewlett-Packard, Pfizer, and the others, but these stocks had surely gotten cheap in a hurry. Our clients' focus on companies prevented a lot of needless worry or panic and helped them make sensible decisions.

To be a winner, *be a student of success.* Analyze why some companies are successful and others are not. Especially, observe successful investors and try to emulate them.

• To manage a portfolio well, it is also very important to *keep up-to-date.* This is easy for professionals and generally for younger people, who don't think much about the past and look to the future with the enthusiasm of youth. However, keeping up-to-date is often difficult for older investors, particularly if their portfolios have done well in earlier years. An investor may get comfortable with a list of stocks showing large gains over cost—even if most of those gains were achieved many years ago and the stocks have seriously underperformed the market more recently. When that happens, it almost always means that the companies involved have also underperformed in terms of growth and profitability. So they should have been reexamined in the light of more recent conditions to see if their long-term fundamentals had deteriorated, as occurred with electric utilities in the early 1990s. At the same time, it's likely that some other industries and companies have strengthened themselves and become more attractive investments (as banks did after 1990). Investors who didn't keep up-to-date missed these important changes.

Staying current doesn't mean chasing every new fad that comes along, but rather reading and listening and talking to knowledgeable people so you are quickly aware of significant changes and important new developments. This takes time and effort—and it requires a lot more than just reading *The Wall Street Journal* over coffee every morning. If an investor can't keep fully in the game, he or she should rely on a professional advisor who is up-to-date.

• Finally, *be a realistic optimist*—and this is not a contradiction in terms. Equity investing does entail some risk—almost all due to the short-term volatility of the stock market—but it requires faith in the future of the U.S. and other economies plus the future of what are currently good industries and companies. Such faith can only be maintained by people who are optimists, at least in the investment area. Unfortunately, some individuals are overly cautious or even pessimistic by nature, making it difficult for them to develop the optimism needed for confidence in the kind of stocks that will provide good long-term results—and thus the willingness to own enough of them. Too often such people want to invest lots of their money in bonds and the rest in slow-growing "safe" companies like utilities or in old names like General Motors that did well for Grandpa but are truly investments of the past.

Of course, as many chapters in this book have shown, overoptimism is deadly. So investors should temper their enthusiasm for the future with a heavy dose of logic and common sense—easy to say, but often hard to do. Realism is essential.

———

When done well, investing is not only rewarding financially, but it is a lot of fun. That's a word I hear more from investors than from people in almost any other type of vocation or avocation. There is great fascination in the process—seeking information, analyzing it, and acting on it. It's also fascinating to watch the results develop, especially over the long term. Obviously, investing isn't fun unless your portfolio does reasonably well—but that is much more probable if you follow a sensible, proven approach like the one discussed in this book. As Warren Buffett has said frequently, it isn't a high IQ that produces superior investment performance, it's rationality and curbing your emotions.

So enjoy investing—it's a great activity, and if you run it sensibly, completing the investment marathon won't leave you way back in the pack all tuckered out.

The Boston Marathon has its infamous Heartbreak Hill, which severely challenges the runners. Long-term investors inevitably will encounter similar obstacles—but those who plan and train well and stay the course will enjoy a "runner's high" as they stride along successfully toward the finish line.

INDEX

About the Author

BRAD PERRY has been a professional investor for nearly fifty years. After graduating from Harvard College and Harvard Business School (where he was a Baker Scholar), he spent eight years as a stock analyst at Loomis, Sayles & Co., a large investment counsel firm based in Boston.

In 1960, he joined David L. Babson & Company, also headquartered in Boston, as a stock analyst. Subsequently, he became director of research for that firm, a portfolio manager, and, in 1978, president. In 1983 he was named chairman of the firm, and since retiring from that position in 1992, he has been a consultant to Babson, which manages $20 billion of investments for pension funds, endowment funds, insurance companies, a group of no-load mutual funds, and individual investors.

Mr. Perry also serves as a consultant to other investment organizations. He has been a prolific writer on investing and a frequent speaker to investment groups, as well as a guest on the television programs *Wall Street Week* and *Adam Smith's Money World.*

In 1985, he received the National Association of Investors Corporation Distinguished Service Award in Investment Education, which cited the clarity and wisdom of his writings and speeches.